# C. G. JUNG AND THE SCIENTIFIC ATTITUDE

# C. G. Jung and the Scientific Attitude

*by*

EDMUND D. COHEN, Ph.D.

PHILOSOPHICAL LIBRARY
New York

# Contents

Preface .......................................... vii

Acknowedgments .................................. xi

1. THE COMPLEX ..................................... 1

2. THE STRUCTURE OF THE PSYCHE AND THE PSYCHOLOGICAL
TYPES ............................................ 12

3. THE COLLECTIVE UNCONSCIOUS AND THE UNIVERSAL FORMS   29

4. JUNG AND THE SCIENTIFIC ATTITUDE ................... 70

5. JUNG'S SOCIAL RELEVANCE ......................... 92

6. JUNG AND ACADEMIC PSYCHOLOGY ..................... 121

7. THE DANGERS OF ANALYTICAL PSYCHOLOGY .............. 138

Appendix I ...................................... 157

Appendix II ..................................... 158

Bibliography ..................................... 161

Index .......................................... 163

# Preface

The psychology of Carl Gustav Jung (1875-1961; pronounced "yoong") is pervaded by paradoxes: A great many people are aware it exists, but exceedingly few have more than a superficial knowledge of it, laced with several very persistent misconceptions. It is scientific in the truest sense of the term, yet its critics charge its author with obscurantism and mysticism. It includes an astonishingly comprehensive model of the structure of the psyche, that lends itself all too easily to being misunderstood as a finished systematic theory, yet harbors an irremediable vagueness and leads to wondering speculation at the frontiers of human knowledge. And although every facet of it is imbued with skepticism and modest regard for the limitations of our knowledge, it attracts disciples who quickly come to profess mastery of the secret of life itself, and make a sort of personal demigod of Jung.

The present work aims to introduce Jung's viewpoint to a readership which, like the author, has been brought up on materialism, positivism, and the view that matters of the spirit are incommensurable with those of science, the latter asserting their truth by giving us power over nature, and the former, their falsity and unreality, representing only so much whistling in the dark on the parts of our poor benighted forebears. The physical science that masters nature, however, also points increasingly to a reality behind its phenomena which is alien to conscious understanding and boggling to the intellect. This same science is a product of the psyche, which also produces art, myth, religious expression, and the best and worst in our social surroundings. Psychology, to be true to its subject matter—the psyche—(and the ultimate aim of any science is fidelity to its subject matter without arbitrary methodological restrictions) must include all these things, and thereby be a focal point of disciplines and a bridge between them. In addition, it must struggle against the distortion of perspective which comes from being itself a part of the whole it attempts to study. A one-sidedly physical science-oriented psychology reduces the psyche to one of the psyche's own several *modi operandi*, which is, of course, ridiculous. Contemporary academic psychologists, often limiting themselves to reductionistic, mechanical explanations, and covering over the nuances of human experience with statistics, seem to me to have all but ceased making progress toward their true objectives. The excuse that theirs is a young science that will increasingly resemble its more mature sisters as time goes by, is wearing thin.

My aim in this book, then, is the rehabilitation of some significant and valid content of a kind which academic psychology has all but overlooked. To be sure, I also discuss some matters Jung was interested in, that have become fashionable and sensational, such as astrology, occult phenomena, *I Ching*, and matters psychedelic. Since Jung's productivity covers a span of more than fifty-five years, his reputation rests largely on earlier statements, upon which he later improved. I have tried to correct the resulting misconceptions, and some others, namely that he was merely an offshoot of Freud, an obscurantist, a mystic, an anti-Semite, a racist, a Nazi-sympathizer, or even a philosopher. Most of all, I wish to correct the misconceptions that he claimed there were inherited memories, reminiscences or the like, and that he was inconsistent or self-contradictory. His work reflects that its subject matter is full of paradoxes and conjunctions of opposites, but what appear to be contradictions turn out, under close scrutiny, not to be so.

Jung's psychology, being an attempt to generalize from experience, is primarily empirical. Since discrepancies between the logical and psychological significances of a thing are the rule rather than the exception, one cannot *deduce* a psychology. Jung would frequently defend his formulations saying, "it is simply so," not meaning to be arbitrary, but referring to his background of experience as their foundation. Accordingly, the extent to which his work sheds light on the inner experience of others is the measure of its validity. On the problem of the validity of his psychology, Jung said:

> I know that what Freud said agrees with many people, and I assume that these people have exactly the kind of psychology that he describes. Adler, who has an entirely different views, also has a large following, and I am convinced that many people have an Adlerian psychology. I too have a following—not so large as Freud's—and it consists presumably of people who have my psychology. I consider my contribution to psychology to be my subjective confession. It is my personal psychology, my prejudice that I see psychological facts as I do. . . . But I expect Freud and Adler to do the same and confess that their ideas are their subjective point of view. So far as we admit our personal prejudice, we are really contributing towards an objective psychology.[1]

After I had settled on the basic outline of this book, it became evident that I had arranged its parts unknowingly in more or less chronological order; this has emphasized to me the inseparability of the process of discovery from the content. I believe it is principally the neglect of the context of Jung's experiences, and of the intellectual and spiritual climate in which he lived, that have made so much of the secondary source material on Jung's psychology fall flat.

I have made liberal use of footnotes to introduce background material, and consider these integral to the book. More references appear than are, strictly speaking, necessary: I hope some readers will find them useful nevertheless.

Many people have helped with this work, and there are a few to whom I am particularly in debt. Mrs. Aniela Jaffé, Dr. Gerhard Adler, and Mr. William McGuire made it possible for me to read

---

[1] Jung, C. G. *Analytical Psychology: Its Theory and Practice.* New York: Pantheon, 1968. p. 140. Not part of the *Collected Works*, this book consists of five lectures Jung gave originally in English to the Tavistock Society in London, in the fall of 1935. It is a superb summary of Jung's thought up to that time, but stresses the superfluous dichotomy of *ectopsyche* vs. *endopsyche*, which he subsequently abandoned.

*C. G. Jung: Letters* prior to its publication, and gave me general encouragement, as did Dr. Marie-Louise von Franz. Professor John Hughes and Mrs. Jo Ann Walker offered many helpful comments that have made this a better work.

Fairfax, Virginia

# ACKNOWLEDGEMENTS

The author and publishers wish to thank the following for permission to quote from various works: Aldus Books Ltd., London (*Man and His Symbols*, edited by C. G. Jung, copyright 1964 by Aldus Books Ltd.); Harper & Row, Publishers, New York (*From the Life and Work of C. G. Jung*, by Aniela Jaffé, copyright 1971 by Harper & Row, Publishers); Holt, Rinehart and Winston, Inc., New York (*I Never Promised You a Rose Garden*, by Hannah Green, copyright 1964 by Holt, Rinehart and Winston, Inc.); Liveright Publishing Corp., New York (*The Place of Value in a World of Facts*, by Wolfgang Köhler, copyright 1965 by Liveright Publishing Corp.); Northwestern University Press, Evanston, Illinois (English-language rights to *Zahl und Zeit*, by Marie-Louise von Franz); Pantheon Books, New York, and Routledge & Kegan Paul, Ltd., London (*Analytical Psychology: Its Theory and Practice*, by C. G. Jung, copyright 1968 by Pantheon Books, and Routledge & Kegan Paul, Ltd.); Pantheon Books, New York, and Collins Publishers, London (*Memories, Dreams, Reflections*, by C. G. Jung, recorded and edited by Aniela Jaffé, translated by Richard and Clara Winston, copyright 1963 by Pantheon Books, and Collins Publishers); Princeton University Press, Princeton, New Jersey, and Routledge & Kegan Paul Ltd., London (*C. G. Jung: Letters*, ed. by Gerhard Adler, in collaboration with Aniela Jaffé, trans. by R. F. C. Hull, Bollingen Series XCV, vol. 1: 1906-1950, vol. 2: 1951-1961, copyright 1973 by Princeton University Press, and *The Collected Works of C. G. Jung*, ed. by G. Adler, M. Fordham, W. McGuire, and H. Read, trans. by R. F. C. Hull, Bollingen Series XX, vol. 1, *Psychiatric Studies*, copyright 1957 by Bollingen Foundation; vol. 2, *Experimental Researchers*, trans. by Leopold Stein, copyright 1973 by Princeton University Press; vol. 3 *The Psychogenesis of Mental Disease*, copyright 1960 by Bollingen Foundation; vol. 4, *Freud and Psychoanalysis*, copyright 1961 by Bollingen Founda-

# CHAPTER 1

# The Complex

"The essential basis of our personality is affectivity."
(C. W., vol. 3, par. 77. *The Psychology of Dementia Praecox*.)[1]

The first major phase of Jung's work centered around the concept of the complex. Though so much time has passed since Jung's last work on it was completed, two points which are the essence of its significance are generally overlooked: 1. The complex provides a model that can account for most of the categories of pathology commonly found in text books of Abnormal Psychology. 2. That model is fairly well supported by experimental evidence. (The later articles on it, where Jung researched relatively minute variations of his association experiment before turning to other things, would not seem out of place in a current number of an American Psychological Association journal.)

Jung worked on the complex at a time when the conflict between science and technology on the one hand, and religion and traditional values on the other, was first becoming acute. Jung had grown up in several rural Swiss towns, the son of a Swiss Reform pastor who was tortured by doubts about his faith and his vocation. As a young man, Jung was interested in both

---

[1] This form is used throughout this work for citations of C. G. Jung's *Collected Works* (New York: Bollingen Foundation, Inc. 1953ff.). Paragraph numbers are used since these are consistent throughout the various English language editions, and page numbers sometimes are not. The addition of the title of the original book or article will provide at least some clues for those who have non-*Collected Works* versions of Jung's writings handy. Citations other than "C.W." are either of selections that will not appear in the *Collected Works*, or may appear in vol. 18, which had not appeared when this work was completed.

the natural sciences and the humanities, experienced these interests as incompatible, and consequently had trouble choosing a profession. The eventual choice of medicine was for practical and economic reasons, not the least of which was the independence a physician could enjoy, in contradistinction to a teacher or researcher.

Although he had often seemed dull to his teachers during his school years (he was a very inward-looking boy, often at variance with what was going on around him), by the time he reached his early twenties he had established himself as a very promising student of physical medicine. He read Krafft-Ebing's *Textbook of Insanity Based on Clinical Observations,* and seeing in it the opportunity to reconcile his divergent interests, was influenced to specialize in psychiatry. His professors reacted to that decision with bewilderment, since psychiatry had little content and less prestige in those days.

Much of his fortunate insight into the nature of the complex, and also the material for his Doctor of Medicine dissertation,[2] came from observing a fifteen-year-old girl, a psychic medium, through whom the spirits of the dead ostensibly spoke. (She also did table tipping, constructed a complicated diagram of the structure of the universe, labelled in a secret language she would reveal to nobody, and showed some other miscellaneous symptoms, including somnambulism.) At the time (1898-1899) Jung's mind was completely closed to the possibility of valid occult phenomena, an attitude that experience later forced him to revise somewhat.

After a rather nondescript childhood, she developed an interest in clairvoyance, which seemed perfectly natural and normal to her. She would go into a trance, and various departed "others" would speak through her: these included a female character named "Ivenes," smarter and more cultivated than the girl herself, the girl's grandfather, and a silly fop named "Ulrich von Gerbenstein," who spoke high German, in contrast to the girl, who spoke only the Basel dialect of Swiss German (there had once been a young man in the household as a guest who had spoken high

---

[2] C. W., vol. 1, 1-165. *On the Psychology of So-Called Occult Phenomena.*

2

German). There were several further variations of these basic characters; all of them were aware of the girl's life and experience, but in her normal, waking state, she was not aware of theirs.

At that time, a number of cases of multiple personality, amnesia, conversion reaction, etc., in short, those which were later classified together by Breuer and Freud in their famous *Studies on Hysteria*, were being reported, albeit lacking the occult twist of this one.[3] The typical explanations were along the lines of "hysterio-epilepsy" or "psychopathic inferiority." Jung principally explained the case as suggestions internalized at an unconscious level (showing, for instance, that the cosmic diagram could have come from hearing Kant's *Natural History and Theory of the Heavens* discussed around her, and that she had known prototypes for her ectoplasmic visitors).

Where this experience with a human personality divided into several relatively independent splinter personalities provided a general background for the concept of the complex, the specific impetus for it came from experimental psychology.[4] Sir Francis Galton had used a word-association test as early as 1884 in his ill-fated "anthropometric laboratory," focussing his attention on the nature of the response words, and their relationship to the stimulus words. Wundt [5] used such a test in a similar way, and G. Aschaffenburg and F. Kramer also worked with word-association tests prior to Jung, all without particularly memorable results.

---

[3] A thorough, documented account of these can be found in Henri Ellenberger's *The Discovery of the Unconscious* (New York: Basic Books, 1970), pp. 141-151.

[4] There have been many instances of cross-fertilization in the early days of fields which later came to have virtually nothing in common. For instance Hermann Ebbinghaus, who practically founded modern learning theory in 1885 with his book, *On Memory*, did his doctoral dissertation on Eduard von Hartmann's *Philosophy of the Unconscious*, a work which came to conclusions astonishingly similar to Freud's, almost forty years before Freud published his first work on Psychoanalysis, and which heavily influenced Jung. Learning theory and Psychoanalysis, different as they now have become, arise in part from the same question: "Where are our thoughts when we are not thinking of them (e.g., are unconscious of them)?"

[5] Wilhelm Wundt (1832-1920) is generally acknowledged as the founding father of academic psychology, having established the world's first experimental psychological laboratory in Leipzig in 1879, and also the defunct school of psychological structuralism. Jung spoke of his work as ". . . an old-

3

Jung, in his use of Wundt's word-association test, carried on the interest in classifying the kinds of responses to everyday words, which had so characterized the earlier work. For instance, he found that uneducated subjects, as well as defective ones, were less superficial and more conditioned by their inner thoughts in their responses, than educated subjects, who may have taken the test less seriously than the uneducated. Distraction of attention while the test was in progress tended to make responses more superficial, and women were more easily distracted (i.e., showed "less ability to divide attention") than men.[6] A great many other aspects of word-association responses were looked at, with results upon which Jung declined to generalize.

Jung's special contribution arose from his noticing that the reaction times were more interesting than the responses themselves.[7] A disturbed response, one with an unusually long reaction time, or in extreme cases, no response at all, signified an emotional disturbance associated with the stimulus word. It is to this that the term "complex" principally refers, and it is the same thing we now popularly call a "hang-up." The test came to have a standardized form (reproduced below in Appendix 1) and technique. The stimulus word list would be responded to twice, with reaction times (measured with a stop watch) and the responses themselves being noted. In the reproduction trial, the subject would be instructed to give the same responses again, if possible, inability to do this also pointing to a disturbance associated with the stimulus word.[8] A disturbed response can point to anything from a mildly embarrassing aspect of the subject's past life, about

---

fashioned kind of psychology . . . that has nothing to do with the details of human life but moves in the stratosphere of abstract ideas." (*Op. cit., Analytical Psychology* . . . , p. 87.) Nevertheless, Wundt's influence is strongly evident in Jung. The irrational functions, and the psychological typology of which they are a part (see ch. 2, below) are reminiscent, at least in style, of Wundt's notion of apperception, and his tridimensional model of feeling, respectively.

6 Jung, C. G. and F. Riklin. "The Associations of Normal Subjects." (C. W., vol. 2, par. 490).

7 C. W., vol. 2, pars. 660-727. "Psychoanalysis and Association Experiments." Also, pars. 793-862. "Association, Dream, and Hysterical Symptom."

8 My treatment of this topic draws heavily on *Die Empire des Unbewussten* by C. A. Meier, (Zürich: Rascher Verlag, 1968).

4

which he could tell us if he were willing, to a genuine neurosis, into which he has no conscious insight. The former would be a case of a conscious complex, the latter, an unconscious one; in practice, the difference between the two is a matter of degree.

Since the word-association test could tap conscious material that the subject was otherwise unwilling to disclose, it was natural for Jung to explore its possible forensic use.[9] As a lie detection procedure, it came to be known as the "evidence experiment" (*Tatbestandsexperiment*). Its nature is most succinctly shown in the following paragraph from an article Jung published in 1905:

> Yesterday evening an elderly gentleman came to see me, obviously in a state of great agitation. He told me that he had staying with him a young man of eighteen, whose guardian he was. Some weeks ago he noticed from time to time that small sums of money were missing from his cashbox, now amounting to over 100 francs. He at once informed the police, but was unable to bring proofs against any one person. He rather suspected his ward. . . . He now asked me to hypnotize the young man and question him under hypnosis. As can readily be understood, I declined this strange request, but proposed instead the association test, which could be rendered plausible enough in the form of a consultation (the suspected delinquent had wanted to consult me once before on account of mild nervous troubles). His guardian agreed . . . and this morning the young man turned up for the consultation. I had, of course, previously equipped my list of one hundred stimulus words with the critical words designed to hit the complex. The experiment went off smoothly; but in order to determine the critical reactions still more precisely I decided to employ my reproduction procedure as well. The complex for the theft was then revealed so plainly by the associations that I was able to tell the young man with quiet assurance: "You have been stealing." He paled, was completely nonplussed for a moment, and after a little hesitation broke down and tearfully admitted to the theft.[10]

Clearly such a test leaves a great deal to the skill and intuition of the tester, and to luck. Because of this, Jung was generally pessimistic about the procedure. Occasionally, after he had stopped

---

[9] C. W., vol. 2, pars. 728-792. "The Psychological Diagnosis of Evidence."
[10] C. W., vol. 1, par. 483. "On the Psychological Diagnosis of Facts."

working with the test, he was called upon to give expert testimony.[11]

While the association experiment contributed little to the modern paraphernalia of lie detection, Jung did some other work which securely establishes him as one of the fathers of the modern lie detector. That work utilized the psychogalvanometer, measuring galvanic skin response (GSR), and the psychopneumograph, measuring respiration rate. (Measurement of blood pressure, pulse rate, and sometimes even brain waves in conjunction with an electroencephalograph, are refinements which have since been added.) Specifically, he found that a sudden shift in GSR was more likely to occur when the stimulus word was associated with an unconscious complex, than a conscious one. Respiration rate, on the other hand, would increase markedly when a conscious complex was hit, and was even apt to be inhibited under the influence of an unconscious one.[12] Accordingly, in a psychotic person, in whom what is unconscious in a normal or neurotic person pours out continuously, sharp accelerations of respiratory rate, and labile GSR responses may result from complex-related stimulus words.[13]

Thus far, we have taken a detailed look at a "normal" case (the thief of the cash box), and a "neurotic" one (the medium who, having an intact ego-personality, would not be considered "psychotic"). To be able to generalize about the behavior of complexes, and define them, we must take up the problem of psychosis, specifically of schizophrenia.

The term "schizophrenia" (lit. "split personality") is almost always misused by non-psychologists, who understand it as meaning a clearly divided personality with two or more well defined aspects. In the conventional psychiatric nomenclature, such a personality is said to exhibit dissociation, or suffer from hysteria. A truly schizophrenic person, however, is more accurately de-

---

[11] C. W., vol. 2, pars. 1357-1388. "On the Psychological Diagnosis of Evidence: The Evidence-Experiment in the Näf Trial."

[12] C. W., vol. 2, pars. 1015-1035. "On the Psychophysical Relations of the Association Experiment."

[13] Ricksher, Charles and Jung, C. G. "Further Investigations on the Galvanic phenomenon and Respiration in Normal and Insane Individuals." (C. W., vol. 2, pars. 1180-1311.)

scribed as having a *shattered*, rather than a split personality. In Jung's words:

> In hysteria the dissociated personalities are still in a sort of interrelation, so that you always get the impression of a total person. With a hysterical case you can establish a rapport, you get a feeling reaction from the whole person. There is only a superficial division between certain memory compartments, but the basic personality is always present. In the case of schizophrenia that is not so. There you encounter only fragments, there is nowhere a whole. Therefore, if you have a friend or a relative whom you have known well and who becomes insane, you will get a tremendous shock when you are confronted with a fragmentary personality which is completely split up. You can only deal with one fragment at a time; it is like a splinter of glass.[14]

A particularly enlightening case, diagnosed by Jung very early in his career with the word-association test, was that of a thirty year old matron, with a young son and a daughter who had died of typhoid fever at age four, hospitalized for schizophrenia with depression. While conventional methods yielded no clue to the causes, there were definite reactions to the words "angel," "obstinate," "evil," "rich," "money," "stupid," "dear," and "marry."

From these Jung was able to piece the story together. She had had a chance to marry a very desirable and rich man, but lost it out of modesty and shyness. Being reminded of it by an old friend when she had been married to another man for five years, had made her regret acute. A very short time after that, she was bathing her children in the not altogether safe water of the town where they lived. When the children wanted to drink the bath water, she let them: a behavior which later seemed unaccountable to her, for she surely knew better. Her daughter—who she thought to be the offspring of a clandestine love affair she had had, and not her husband's child— died of typhoid from drinking the infected water. Thus, the mother was a murderess. After much indecision, and then only because the bad prognosis of the case called for decisive action, Jung told her point blank: "You killed your child." This sent her into an emotional state, but inside of

---

[14] *Op. cit.*, Analytical Psychology . . . p. 112.

three weeks she was well enough to be discharged, and in fifteen years of follow-up, had no relapse. Having faced up to her guilt, she was able to bear it, where, as a dreaded secret from her awareness, its effect on her had been devastating.[15]

But what have complexes to do with this? How is it that they are the common denominator of the three very dissimilar cases? Jung defines complexes as "constellations of psychic elements grouped around feeling-toned contents. . . ."[16] The vagueness of the term "psychic elements" is intentional and necessary. "Psychic elements" can be thoughts, feelings, images, reminiscences, urges, or interests, to name a few possibilities. They overlap extensively in meaning, and are convertible into one another (just how much so, we will see in ch. 3). An attribute they share in common is that they are composed of psychic energy, or *libido*. Jung conceived of libido as a *universally convertible energetic resource* of the psyche. It is quite different from Freud's conception, in which libido is basically erotic or destructive, all other applications being inefficient derivatives of the two.[17] The Freudian view of interest in, or motivation towards a thing as investment of libido in it is, however, retained. "It really denotes *subjective intensity* [italics in original]. Anything potent, any content highly charged with energy. . . ."[18]

A complex, then, is a grouping of energy-laden psychic contents which are compatible and belong together. It has coherent set of values and objectives (e.g., its feeling tone). If it is prominent enough to include a sizable share of the personality's energy, it takes on a personality of its own, and possibly even its own consciousness. Thus the ego-personality[19] is itself a complex, and the

---

[15] *Ibid.*, pp. 58-61.

[16] C. W., vol. 8, par. 18. "On Psychic Energy."

[17] Freud's model, with its well defined structures of ego and superego channeling libido, is far more clear and explicit than Jung's with its multifaceted constellations with feeling-toned centers. Between the two, it is a question of whether it is better to have a well elaborated system that goes beyond the data, or a tentative idea that accords with what little is known about an elusive object of study.

[18] C. W., vol. 5, par. 238. *Symbol of Transformation.*

[19] N. B.: The terms "Ego" and "Self" have different meanings in Jung's work than in psychology generally. (These are explained in chs. 2 and 3.) The Jungian usages do not, however, contradict the dictionary definitions of

most important one. When a person is particularly complex-ridden, the energy available to the ego-personality is reduced. A neurotic person's symptoms can be better understood as the manifestations of complexes (splinter personalities) competing with the ego-personality for control. These were articulated with rare clarity in the "ectoplasmic visitors" of Jung's psychic medium. In the schizophrenic woman, the complex attracted so much energy from the ego-personality as to cripple it; when the complex could be integrated with the conscious attitude, the ego-personality could reestablish itself. In the "normal" there are complexes, but these are not powerful enough to cause serious trouble.

The complex model can be compared to a parliament: In a "normal" person there is a ruling party (the ego-personality), and a reasonably loyal opposition (composed of the complexes) that offers some resistance and gains some concessions. In a neurotic person, there is also a ruling party, but with a stubborn, disruptive opposition, possibly due in part to excessive rigidity and too few concessions from the ruling party. In the schizophrenic, no party is able to form a government, and confusion reigns. This analogy holds for the explanation why complexes become unconscious. If they are too incompatible with the conscious attitude, are at cross purposes with it, they withdraw on their own from its presence. They are not *repressed*, as in Freud's model; they are *dissociated*.

> . . . there are any number of cases where it is impossible to show, even with the most careful examination, the slightest trace of "putting aside" or of conscious repression, and where

---

the terms. For clarity, I capitalize them when I use them in the Jungian sense, and avoid using them in their general psychology constructions, except in hyphenated combinations such as "ego-personality." (This is a device Jung could not have exploited, since all nouns are capitalized in German.)

I see two main reasons for the existence of this confusion, which probably could not have been avoided: 1. The two concepts evolved gradually over the years; the terms are often used in the conventional way, or ambiguously in the earlier works. It would be possible in all good faith for someone to write a treatise "proving" Jung intellectually incompetent by demonstrating discrepancies without taking development over time into account. 2. The German terms *Ich* (lit. "I") for "Ego," and *Selbst* for "Self" (the reflexive pronoun being *sich*) lend themselves to the misunderstanding far less. This is an area where Jung's work is particularly vulnerable to losing something in translation.

it seems as if the process of repression were more in the nature of a passive disappearance, or even as if the impressions were dragged beneath the surface by some force operating from below.[20]

Thus, in Jung's model, dissociation (of psychic contents from the ego-personality) is the fundamental pathological mechanism, and repression (voluntarily, or by a censoring mechanism such as Freud's superego), a special case of it, which takes place when the incompatibility of the conscious attitude and the complex is particularly acute. In Freud's model, repression by the reified agent of the superego, is the main mechanism, and dissociation, the special case. It is not for nothing that in modern slang, an effective, psychologically healthy person is referred to as "together."

The model also finds credence in the following much-quoted passage from Hermann Hesse's *Steppenwolf*:

> The breast and the body are indeed one, but the souls that dwell in it are not two, nor five, but countless in number. Man is an onion made up of a hundred integuments, a texture made up of many threads. The ancient Asiatics knew this well enough, and in the Buddhist Yoga an exact technique was devised for unmasking the illusion of the personality. The human merry-go-round sees many changes: the illusion that cost India the efforts of thousands of years to unmask is the same illusion that the West has labored just as hard to maintain and strengthen.[21]

With the complex model, then, we set beyond what conventional psychopathology can show us about neurosis and schizophrenic psychosis. To the extent we have covered it, it does not account for paranoia or for the "character disorders," though, as we shall see in the next chapter, it can account for them. More importantly, the complex-model phase of Jung's work gave the autonomy of the complexes too much emphasis. They occur, after all, in the same organism, and therefore must have an intimate and systematic relationship to one another: this is the central question of the next

---

[20] C. W., vol. 4, par. 212. *The Theory of Psychoanalysis.*
[21] New York: Modern Library, 1963, pp. 66-67.

chapter, and accordingly, of the second phase of Jung's work. Another vital question is that of how it happens that undifferentiated psychic energy comes to have a specific structure, and what the nature of that structure is. That question occupied the third phase of Jung's work, and the second half of his life; we will skim the surface of it in chapter 3.

CHAPTER 2

# The Structure of the Psyche and the Psychological Types

"Science must serve; it errs when it usurps the throne." (C. W., vol. 13, par. 2. "Commentary on 'The Secret of the Golden Flower.'")

During the first phase of his work, Jung had been a staff physician at the famous Burghölzli hospital in Zürich, the assistant of Eugen Bleuler,[1] who provided a great deal of encouragement and support for his early work. From this position, Jung passed into private practice, and into his well known relationship with Sigmund Freud (1856-1939). Jung knew of Freud through *Studies on Hysteria*, and *The Interpretation of Dreams*. The compatibility of the findings of the word association experiment with Freud's hypothesis of the unconscious prompted Jung to write to him, and send him a copy of *The Psychology of Dementia Praecox*. Jung first met Freud in Vienna in 1907, and this resulted in a close friendship, collaboration in a wide range of professional activities, and their trip to America in 1909.[2] Jung rose to a pre-

---

[1] Eugen Bleuler (1857-1939) was very influential in psychiatric circles before the advent of psychoanalysis, and was one of the first to give Freud's work a favorable hearing. The various editions of his *Lehrbuch der Psychiatrie* were instrumental in disseminating psychoanalytic ideas in general psychiatry.

[2] At the invitation of G. Stanley Hall, they attended the twentieth anniversary celebration of Clark University in Worcester, Massachusetts, along with Ernest Jones and Sandor Ferenczi. There, they met almost all the psychological luminaries of that day, including William James, Edward Bradford Titchener, and James McKeen Cattell. Jung mastered English (which Freud never did), returned to America a number of times, and had abundant interchange with English speaking people throughout his life.

eminent position in Freud's psychoanalytic [3] movement, and became president of the International Psychoanalytic Society, and editor of one of its two main publications, *Jahrbuch*. As Jung began to develop his own ideas, his relations with the Freudians became increasingly strained.[4] Jung identifies the publication of *Psychology of the Unconscious* [5] as the precipitating factor in the break with Freud: ". . . all my friends and acquaintances dropped away. My book was declared to be rubbish: I was a mystic, and that settled the matter." [6]

While Jung was no mystic, his work developed along lines so different from Freud's as to make me think it inaccurate to call his work a variation of Freud's. The difference stems, first of all, from the dissimilarity of the two men's backgrounds. Freud was the first member of his family to overcome the barriers to advancement which Jews faced in central Europe in those days. He rebelled against the Jewish traditions which alienated him from his European surroundings, and his materialism and positivism were vehicles for that rebellion. He forthrightly sought to reduce the psyche to physiology, and seriously expected that physiological structures corresponding to his id, ego, and superego would someday be found. Thus he sought to subordinate the humanities to the natural sciences; his work was inconoclastically polemic against art, religion, and morality, reducing these to mere byproducts of repression. His movement attracted, with rare exceptions, persons from similar situations. So scarce were gentiles in

---

[3] The terms "psychoanalysis" and "psychoanalytic" were appropriated by Freud as referring to his particular school. Accordingly, Jung and Adler eventually chose the rubrics "Analytical Psychology" and "Individual Psychology" to identify their respective schools. Today the term "psychoanalysis" is often construed to mean any psychology of the unconscious, and Freud's school in particular is referred to as "orthodox psychoanalysis."

[4] Some sources on this period are: Jung, C. G. *Memories, Dreams, Reflections*, Recorded and Edited by Aniela Jaffé (New York: Vintage Books, 1965), pp. 146-169. A more detailed account, heavily biased in favor of Freud is Jones, Ernest. *The Life and Work of Sigmund Freud*, vol. 2 (New York: Basic Books, 1953), pp. 67-167. A relatively even-handed account (mildly hostile to both Jung and Freud) is Brome, Vincent. *Freud and His Early Circle* (New York: Morrow & Co., 1967), pp. 39-41.

[5] Later extensively revised and retitled *Symbols of Transformation* (C. W., vol. 5).

[6] *Op. cit., Memories, Dreams, Reflections*, p. 167.

the International Psycho-analytic Society that Freud was glad to have Jung be prominent in it, in order to protect psychoanalysis from "the danger of becoming a Jewish national affair."[7]

Jung, while the son of a poor country parson, had a background of traditional, humanistic learning.[8] Since he had not experienced the special estrangement a Jew feels when he grows up and receives his education among gentiles, since his orientation toward traditional religious values was far less negative than Freud's, and since he was far better versed in philosophy and *belles lettres* than Freud,[9] naturally his attitude was different. Under the influence of a more or less even division of his loyalties between science and humanism, he sought to reconcile the two.

The essence of the difference is shown by the rôle each viewpoint assigns to the *symbol* in human thought. For Freud, the psyche was clearly divided into the unconscious, where the primary id processes of infantile erotic, incestuous, and destructive impulses were repressed by the reified agent of the superego; and the conscious, where the rational, reality-oriented thought processes of the ego took place. The latter made some gratification of id impulses possible, in compromise with morality and reality. The superego also censored threatening memories from the conscious, i.e. those too dangerous or immoral for the ego to tolerate; most strongly censored were memories repressed since early in life. The symbolism of dreams, religion, and art works represented a diluted, depotentiated form of the terrible, taboo products of

---

[7] Op. cit., Jones, p. 48. From a letter by Freud to Karl Abraham in 1909, exact date not given.

[8] Jung had been named after his illustrious grandfather, C. G. Jung the Elder (1794-1864), who had been rector of the University of Basel, and was rumored to be an illegitimate son of Johan Wolfgang von Goethe (1749-1832), the most famous author in the German language, and bore a striking physical resemblance to him. Jung the Elder had originally come from Germany, where he had made himself unwelcome by a very distant association with student rebellion.

[9] Jung said, ". . . I had the impression that Freud's intellectual history began with Büchner [an early nineteenth century German realist playwright], Moleschott, Du Bois-Reymond [early materialist-reductionist physiologists], and Darwin." (Op. cit., Memories, Dreams, and Reflections, p. 161). Also, Freud was only vaguely familiar with Nietzsche (Op. cit., Jones, p. 344); it would be comparable for a contemporary person to be only vaguely familiar with Sartre or B. F. Skinner.

14

the id. So disguised, these could come to consciousness and be integrated with the ego, one sub-lethal dose at a time.

Symbolism, then, played a rôle subservient to that of rational thinking in Freud's view. Art became a last resort of the neurotic, and religion, a collective control of the socially unacceptable in man. Analysis became an interminable, distasteful process, since man's dreaded secrets were great, and his ability to face them, small. Inability or reluctance to accept the somber insights of a Freudian analysis was termed "resistance." It became customary for psychoanalysts to be dogmatic, and absolve themselves of the responsibility to consider, on its merits, criticism of their work, by diagnosing it as "resistance" on the part of the critic.[10]

For Jung, the symbol [11] was the *sine qua non* of the psyche, conscious and unconscious. Accordingly, he placed much more emphasis than Freud on dreams and spontaneous artistic production, in understanding an individual person. A symbol is *a representation* or *expression of a partially unconscious psychic state*. In defining "psychic state," the same difficulty returns which rendered our discussion of "psychic contents" vague. A psychic state can be a perception, an emotion, an insight, an intuition, or a desire, to name a few possibilities. It can be totally intrapsychic, or can involve some physical occurrence to which the psyche responds. A symbol serves to make knowable and communicable that which cannot be fully explicated or analyzed, that which is known tacitly and implicitly rather than explicitly—e.g.,

---

[10] This authoritarian tendency, sharply contrasting the claim of psychoanalysis to be a science, played a role in the break between Freud and Jung. In 1910, Freud said to Jung, ". . . Promise me never to abandon the sexual theory. That is the most essential thing of all. You see, we must make a dogma of it, an unshakable bulwark." Jung asked, "A bulwark—against what?" Freud answered, "Against the black tide of mud . . . of occultism." This exchange had been brought on by Freud's refusal to cooperate with Jung's attempt to interpret one of Freud's dreams, saying, "But I cannot risk my authority!" In Jung's words, "Freud was placing personal authority above truth." (*Op. cit., Memories, Dreams, Reflections*, pp. 150-158).

[11] Jung devoted relatively little effort to defining what a symbol is, probably because the topic had already been discussed exhaustively in German philosophy. I find it best suits the purposes of this work to go to a little beyond Jung's statements on it. I owe a particular debt to Joseph Royce's *The Encapsulated Man* (New York: D. Van Nostrand, 1964), and Ernst Cassierer's *An Essay on Man* (New Haven: Yale U. Press, 1944).

15

unconsciously. A symbol goes beyond its referent, yet is an incomplete representation of it. It has an integral, organic relationship with its referent, and a one-to-many relationship to it. (Thus, a symbol may refer to one of those class concepts where everybody can tell what is a member of the class and what is not, but nobody can satisfactorily say what the defining characteristic of the class is; for example, "living being," and "good.")

We symbolize those things about which, in the words of Michael Polanyi, "*we can know more than we can tell*" [his italics].[12] Since it is incomplete and developing, a symbol has a life of its own: once fully explicated, or made fully conscious, a symbol is worn out or dead. Any person who has ever enjoyed a work of art, and through it shared with the artist a knowledge that neither could adequately have explained, knows what a symbol is and what its use is. A symbol is a differentiation of the psyche, which, without it would be undifferentiated in some respect. This is, itself, symbolized in the Biblical creation myth, where the differentiation of the world begins with the division of the primordial chaos into heaven and earth by means of a firmament. (So, a *myth* is a series or progression of symbols expressive of a common large, complex referent.)

A *sign*, in contradistinction to a symbol, represents something explicit, and does so arbitrarily. A sign has a one-to-one relationship to its referent. Mathematics and formal logic are sign systems, or nearly so. Jung cautions us that many representations which display attributes of their referents may seem to be symbols, but really only be signs.[13] Such items include flags, insignia, and coats of arms. A symbol, then, must be relatively spontaneously produced, rather than contrived.

Once we conceive of the psyche as a field of energy, differentiated, segregated, and structured into symbols, on one level, and into complexes, on another, we come to the search for principles of organization of the contents of the psyche, as the next step. Much of the impetus for Jung's taking this step came from his thoughts about the differences among Freud, Adler, and himself. Eros, or sexuality, had been the central motive force in

<hr>

[12] *The Tacit Dimension.* New York: Doubleday, 1966, p. 4.
[13] C. W., vol. 6, par. 817. *Psychological Types.*

16

Freud's viewpoint, until he found it necessary to include what he supposed to be its opposite, Thanatos, the death wish. But Adler made the will to power his first principle, and thereby led Jung to the following observation: "Logically, the opposite of love is hate, and of Eros, Phobos (fear); but psychologically it is the will to power. Where love reigns, there is no will to power; and where the will to power is paramount, love is lacking." [14] Thus, logical and psychological opposites need not correspond. Only empirically can the question of psychological opposites be settled.

It is with this question of opposites that the second phase of Jung's work, dating back to the period around 1920 and culminating in the book *Psychological Types*,[15] was occupied. Jung drew on literary and philosophical examples, and on clinical experience (of which he had amassed a great deal by that time) as data about the behavior of psychological opposites.

Probably the best known result of that period is the opposites dimension *introversion-extraversion*. The two terms have become a part of everyday speech, and since most people use them essentially correctly, little explanation of them should be necessary. James' distinction between tender-mindedness and tough-mindedness [16] and Goethe's principle of systole and diastole (which involves a rhythm or harmony between the two) [17] were part of their background, as was the Freud-Adler contrast:

> Certainly both investigators see the subject in relation to the object; but how differently this relation is seen! With Adler the emphasis is placed on a subject who, no matter what the object, seeks his own security and supremacy; with Freud the emphasis is placed wholly upon objects, which, according to their specific character, either promote or hinder the subject's desire for pleasure.[18]

Adler, then, wrote a psychology of introversion, in contrast to Freud's extraverted one. Accordingly, Freud was greatly concerned

---

[14] C. W., vol. 7, par. 78. *Two Essays*. . . .
[15] C. W., vol. 6. An earlier English language edition, translated by M. D. Eder, was published in the twenties; it was then out of print until 1971.
[16] *Ibid.*, pars. 505-541.
[17] *Ibid.*, par. 428.
[18] C. W., vol. 7, par. 59. *Two Essays*. . . .

with love objects, and the cathection of libido to them; Jung accepted that explanation, and complemented it with another, in which one's libido flows inward toward oneself in a valid style of adaptation to life, and not only in infantile or narcisstic life styles, as Freud implied; ". . . introversion and extraversion are not traits of character at all, but mechanisms, which can, as it were, be switched on or off at will. Only from their habitual predominance do the corresponding characters develop." [19]

Where the extravert moves toward the object in order to increase the degree of stimulation he derives from it, the introvert starts with too much stimulation, and, seeking a way to cope with it, has a problem that never arises for the extravert. Jung quotes Schiller in formulating that problem: "Externalize all within and shape everything without." [20] The idea must exert some control over the object, and so idealistic philosophical viewpoints and emphasis on the abstract properties of a thing are facets of the introverted mechanism. Conversely, it is the object which is seen as exerting control over the idea for the extravert, and empiristic philosophical viewpoints and empathy (understanding a person or thing by imagining oneself in his or its place) characterize the extraverted mechanism. Jung paraphrases Worringer in regarding the difference between Oriental and Occidental viewpoints as explicable in terms of *abstraction* and *empathy*:

> . . . it is precisely the Oriental art-forms and religious that display this abstracting attitude to the world. To the Oriental, therefore, the world must appear very different from what it does to the Occidental, who animates it with his empathy. For the Oriental, the object is imbued with life from the start and has ascendency over him; therefore he withdraws into a world of abstraction. [21]

Where the attitude types of introversion and extraversion are widely known and well understood, the four functions which make up the rest of the typology are little known, and then usually misunderstood. These accounted for a great many things

---

[19] C. W., vol. 6, par. 479. *Psychological Types.*
[20] *Ibid.*, par. 149.
[21] *Ibid.*, par. 494.

Jung had observed in his clinical experience. Represented as the extremes of two related dimensions, the four functions of thinking, feeling, sensation, and intuition can be diagrammed thus:

Thinking

Sensation        +        Intuition

Feeling

If a third axis, representing introversion and extraversion, is imagined passing through the intersection of the lines at right angles to the page, then the entire psychological typology is condensed into a model.

By *thinking* Jung referred to every sort of mental activity that involves an *objective* viewpoint. Thus, logical deduction, ratiocination, induction, judgment, and comparison are all forms of thinking. In practice it will be found that the higher the concious development of this function, the more undifferentiated and unconscious its psychological opposite, feeling, must be.

*Feeling* is all that involves a *subjective* viewpoint toward the object, i.e. valuing it. The goodness or badness, value or worthlessness, and pleasantness or distastefulness of something *to the subject* are the elements of feeling in this sense. Feeling and emotion are only distantly related insofar as the psychological types are concerned, since emotion is a fairly specific phenomenon that does not fit into any general scheme devised by Jung. Thinking and feeling are designated *rational* functions by Jung, since they are both kinds of *reflection*.

A realization of the reciprocity of thinking and feeling is found in a general observation I have heard many non-Jungian clinicians make: When a highly intellectually differentiated person (one in a profession, or with an advanced degree) develops a neurosis, his symptoms will typically be in the area of feeling. He is in inner turmoil, and recognizes inability to know how to relate to people and things as the content of his difficulties. It would be typical of a thinking type to suffer from an existential neurosis. Similarly, a person who characteristically relates to the other in terms of value (often a person in a manual occupation or a housewife) will describe thoughts that are out of control and alien to his concept of himself, as his trouble. In each case it is the undifferentiated and relatively unconscious function that provides the complex with weapons to use against the ego-personality.

The rational functions even provided Jung with some insight into the problem of national character:

> A little while ago I had a nice evening in Paris. Some very cultivated men had invited me, and we had a pleasant conversation. They asked me about national differences, and I thought I would put my foot in it, so I said: 'What you value is la clarté de l'esprit latin. That is because your thinking is inferior. The Latin thinker is inferior in comparison to the German thinker.' They cocked their ears, and I said: 'But your feeling is unsurpassable, it is absolutely differentiated.' They said: 'How is that?' I replied: 'Go to a café or a vaudeville or a place where you hear songs and stage-plays and you will notice a very peculiar phenomenon. There are any number of very grotesque and cynical things and then suddenly something sentimental happens. A mother loses her child, there is a lost love, or something marvellously patriotic, and you must weep. For you, the salt and the sugar have to go together. But a German can stand a whole evening of sugar only. The Frenchman must have some salt in it. You meet a man and say: Enchanté de faire votre connaissance. You are not enchanté de faire sa connaissance at all; you are really feeling: Oh go to the devil. But you are not disturbed, nor is he. But do not say to a German: Enchanté de faire votre connaissance, because he will believe it. A German will sell you a pair of sock-suspenders and not only expect, as is natural, to be paid for it. He also expects to be loved for it.' The German nation is characterized by the fact that its feeling function is inferior, it is not differentiated. If you say that to a German he is offended. I should be offended too. He is very attached to what calls Gemütlichkeit. A room full of smoke in which everybody loves everybody—that is gemütlich and that must not be disturbed. . . . That is la clarté germanique du sentiment, and it is inferior.[22]

Sensation and intuition are designated the *irrational* functions, since they are both kinds of *perception*. *Sensation* refers to the gross, macroscopic aspects of perception. The sensation type is well adapted to the reality of things around him; he deals in facts,

---

[22] Op. cit., Analytical Psychology. . . ., pp. 51-52.

and in the explicit characteristics of things. Stable, orderly surroundings are his preference.

*Intuition* refers to the tacit, subliminal aspects of perception. Where the sensation type is best at dealing with facts, the intuitive type distinguishes himself when there are insufficient facts, when there is an ambiguous situation to be coped with. He is not consciously aware to what in the stimulus situation he responds, but he responds adaptively, nevertheless: it is as if he could see around corners. The intuitive type may possess artistic sensitivities, but need not necessarily. If so, it will be precisely the sensual expression that will fascinate him, since that is the underdifferentiated, problem area for him. The executive who makes important decisions for which there are no satisfactory criteria, and thrives where others would get ulcers, is another example of an intuitive type, as is the drifter who easily adjusts to (and needs) constant change of surroundings.

In every case, there is a *main function* which is the most differentiated and under conscious control, and an *inferior function*— necessarily the psychological opposite of the main function— which is most unconscious, and a stumbling block to the ego-personality. With that qualification, any ordering of functions adding up to a personality type is possible. For general descriptions of the eight (i.e., $2^3$) basic types, I refer the reader elsewhere.[23] In such a condensed survey as this work attempts to be, a list of descriptions would degenerate into a psychological cookbook: this is devoutly to be avoided. Jung said, "People often ask me, 'Now is So-and-So not a thinking type?' I say 'I never thought about it,' and I did not. It is no use at all putting people into drawers with different labels." [24] Knowing the unique person is the essential thing, and knowing his type, merely an aid thereto.

Conscious and unconscious represent still another pair of opposites. They are of little use in a typology, since they would only differentiate a few extreme pathological cases from the rest. They are a unique pair, as they are opposites related to each other

---

[23] C. W., vol. 6, pars. 556-671. *Psychological Types.* Also, von Franz, Marie-Louise. "The Inferior Function." In: *Lectures on Jung's Typology.* New York: Spring Publications, 1971, pp. 22-53.
[24] Op. cit., *Analytical Psychology . . .*, p. 19.

by all the other opposites. The inferior function, being more unconscious than the others, but, to be sure, also conscious to a considerable extent, is the means by which unconscious contents can be related to consciousness. If all four functions could be developed equally, they would all simply be conscious, and the ego-personality would be like a ship adrift in a sea of unconsciousness, with no means of getting its bearings. If they were all totally developed, we would reach a God-like perfection in which there would be no unconsciousness: this is not possible in finite, mortal humans. A certain one-sidedness is necessary for there to be an ego-personality.

Jung got much of his original insight into the relationship of the ego-personality to the unconscious from the following dream he had early in his student years:

> It was night in some unknown place, and I was making slow and painful headway against a mighty wind. Dense fog was flying along everywhere. I had my hands cupped around a tiny light which threatened to go out at any moment. Everything depended on my keeping this little light alive. Suddenly I had the feeling that something was coming up behind me. I looked back and saw a gigantic black figure following me. But at the same moment I was conscious, in spite of my terror, that I must keep my little light going through night and wind, regardless of all dangers. . . . When I awoke . . . I knew . . . that this little light was my conciousness, the only light I have. . . . Though infinitely small and fragile in comparison with the powers of darkness, it is still a light, my only light.[25]

Firstly, the dream literally shows the process of *projection*, with the shadow cast by consciousness. Like dissociation, projection was one of Freud's original ego-defense mechanisms, and took on an altered and greater significance in Jung's viewpoint. When one projects, one experiences ones own psychic contents as external

---

[25] Op. cit., *Memories, Dreams, Reflections*, pp. 87-88. A dream showing the ego-personality in such a precarious situation could point to a latent or prospective psychosis. Jung did have a period later (from about 1912 to 1917) when he had strange, schizophrenia-like inner experiences, and his involvement in work and study reached a much lower ebb than at any time thereafter. This "fallow" period provided much of the insight for his later work.

reality. Psychic contents (or symbols) provide order and interpretation for external stimuli, which is to say that no sense could be made of the evidence of our senses without projection. Jung's pupil, Marie-Louise von Franz, shows that scientific understanding is no exception:

> Although up to now little notice has been taken of Jung's views, today basic research in the sciences has already largely approximated his understanding, since it is now generally known that scientific understanding is based on the formation of "thought-models" in the investigator; nevertheless, *the preconscious prehistory of the occurrence of the thought model*, which is observable in dreams, *is, as a rule, not yet more closely scrutinized*, and accordingly the aspect of projection that goes with every thought-model is today still widely ignored. The incidence of projection is supposedly connected with the . . . mirror-symmetrical relationship of the ego-complex to the center of the unconscious personality. With this relationship is connected the capacity of our consciousness for *reflection* (!), from which all higher consciousness arises. [all italics in original] [26]

It is only a passive form of projection, then, that makes us see the proverbial mote in the eye of our brother because we cannot see the beam that is really in our own. Dr. von Franz sees four levels of consciousness at which projection can take place: [27]

1. Archaic identity. The environment is endowed with every manner of human intention and emotion the perceiver himself experiences. This is the famous (and controversial) *participation mystique* (mystical participation) of the anthropologist Lévy-Bruhl, to whom Jung referred.[28] 2. Naïve belief in the accuracy of the perception. Subject and object are better differentiated than in the first, primitive level. 3. Differentiation between the projected image and the object. The discrepancy between them is attributed to mistake or illusion. 4. Recognition that the content belonging to the image and not the object comes from within one's own

---

[26] C. G. Jung: *Sein Mythos in unserer Zeit*. Frauenfeld CH: Huber Verlag, 1972. pp. 99-100. (My translation of the passage into English.)
[27] *Ibid.*, pp. 98-99.
[28] See C. W., vol. 14, footnote accompanying par. 337. *Mysterium Coniunctionis*.

personality. (If this cannot be proved, and the perceiver suspects that other factors are operating, a sort of reversion to the first level is possible.)

Secondly, the dream shows the fluctuating quality of consciousness. Jung's thoughts in this area were heavily influenced by Pierre Janet[29] who conceived of consciousness as a kind of mental tension, and neurosis as a chronic reduction of that tension. When a decrease in consciousness (*abaissement de niveau mental*) takes place, the individual reverts to a more primitive sort of behavior which originates from the unconscious, the contents of which then have enough energy relatively to become manifest. Such swamping of the conscious with unconscious contents, Jung termed, *invasion*. Invasion is said to take place when one is overcome by a thought or emotion alien to his conscious attitude. When it takes place, one may act out of character, and have cause to say, "I was not myself," or "I don't know what came over me, what got into me, what possessed me." As a fleeting occurrence, possession of the ego-personality by a complex is normal when the energy of the ego-complex is at a low ebb. Individuals are particularly prone to this release and acting out of unconscious contents when in a crowd, so invasion is the underlying phenomenon in mass hysteria (which we will take up in depth in ch. 5).

A fluctuation of consciousness complementary to invasion is *inflation*. Instead of overwhelming consciousness, unconscious contents that really do not belong to it are adopted by it, and it becomes puffed up or "inflated" with them. A person affected by inflation professes ability, skill, understanding, profundity, importance, etc., which he lacks, and is also lacking in self-criticism. Rather than being mastered by him, the contents exert a disruptive fascination on him. Overidentification with the persona (see second paragraph below) is also a form of inflation.

Thirdly, in the dream, the person himself is somehow in the

---

[29] (1859-1947) Jung studied with him in Paris in the winter of 1902-1903. Janet probably deserves credit as the discoverer of the neuroses, having been the first to describe dissociation, hysteria, and feelings of inferiority (*sentiments d'incomplétude*). Later there were bad feelings between Freud and Janet, who felt Freud had usurped recognition rightfully belonging to him.

way of the light of his own consciousness, and a big shadow is cast behind him. This points to a problematical situation, likely to have caused the careful reader some confusion in the foregoing discussion; namely that consciousness and the ego-personality are not quite identical. To reduce that confusion, we must take up the Jungian concept of the Ego.[30]

First, the Ego must not be confused with the persona. The persona (from the Greek word for "mask") is the appearance one presents to others in order to meet their requirements, and insure that one's own needs will be met.[31] At best, it represents a conscious compromise between the constraints of reality, and the need to develop one's own, true, authentic personality. At its worst, it can represent a deceit of oneself and others, that takes an ever-increasing amount of energy to make good. In such a case, we say the Ego is too strongly identified with the persona. It is commonplace for persons whose energies are taken up with a magnificent public image to be thought of as weak, irritable, and infantile by those close to them at home. The wife of the famous German politician Otto von Bismarck once referred to him as "the poor sick worm."

The concept of the Ego evolved parallel with Jung's personal psychic development, so as to stress increasingly the Ego's involvement in making unconscious contents known, at least indirectly. When Jung gave the Tavistock Lectures in 1935, he used a visual model depicting a dark side to the Ego, equal in importance to the light, fully conscious side:

> There . . . we do not see into it, we are an enigma to ourselves. . . . Therefore we are always discovering something new about ourselves. Almost every year something new turns up which we did not know before. We always think we are now at the end of our discoveries. We never are. We go on discovering that we are this, that, and other things, and sometimes we have astounding experiences. That shows there

---

[30] See above, ch. 1, footnote 19.

[31] The persona has been treated as if it were the entirety of the personality by the symbolic interactionist sociologists George H. Mead and Charles H. Cooley. Such a view is indicative of an extraverted view of things. An immensely popular contemporary piece in that vein is Goffman, Erving. *The Presentation of Self in Everyday Life.* (New York: Doubleday, 1959).

is always a part of our personality which is still unconscious, which is still becoming; we are unfinished; we are growing and changing. . . . The ego is like a moving frame on a film. The future personality is not yet visible, but we are moving along, and presently we come to view the future being. *These potentialities naturally belong to the dark side of the ego.* [my italics][32]

By 1950, the rôle of the Ego as synthesizer of conscious and unconscious was more explicitly seen:

> . . . on the one hand the ego rests on the *total field of consciousness*, and on the other, on the *sum total of unconcious contents*. These fall into three groups: first, temporarily subliminal contents that can be reproduced voluntarily (memory); second, unconscious contents that cannot be reproduced voluntarily; third, contents that are not capable of becoming conscious at all. Group two can be inferred from the spontaneous irruption of subliminal contents into consciousness. Group three is hypothetical, it is a logical inference from the facts underlying group two. It contains contents which have *not yet* irrupted into consciousness, or which never will.
> When I said that the ego "rests" on the total field of consciousness I do not mean that it *consists* of this. Were that so, it would be indistinguishable from the field of consciousness as a whole. The ego is only the latter's point of reference, grounded on and limited by the somatic factor. . . . [italics in original][33]

If knowledge of the unconscious is to be gained, then, consciousness must look inward, toward a deeper center. It must adopt an attitude of openness and receptivity (which is fundamental to both eastern meditation techniques and western prayer). Since the insights that occur to it are often fragmentary, inference is an integral part of the attainment of self-knowledge. The Ego, then, represents the level of development of self-knowledge a personality has attained at a particular time—but not the total personality.

To deal with the admittedly hypothetical total personality which can never become fully conscious, we must allow teleolog-

---

[32] Op. cit., Analytical Psychology. . ., pp. 21-22.
[33] C. W., vol. 9¹¹, pars. 4-5 Aion.

ical thought as an admissible alternative of the psyche, and of life generally.[34] The influence of Plato, for whom reality existed to approximate an eternal, perfect ideal, appears here. In the dichotomy between teleological and causal thought, we encounter one of the paradoxical pairs of opposites—of which psyche vs. body, good vs. evil, and finite vs. infinite are others—which want for synthesis as life unfolds. "What to the causal view is *fact* to the final view is *symbol,* and vice versa. Everything that is real and essential to the one is unreal and inessential to the other." [italics in original][35]

To synthesize all the opposites would be tantamount to attaining perfection. A finite mortal cannot do that, so the more modest goal of *completeness* is relevant. The condition of complete, fully developed authenticity toward which an individual life moves, unevenly, increasingly slowly and deliberately with age, and without ever reaching it, is the *Self*. Where the Ego is the total psyche at some particular time, the Self is its totality for all time. Projected, the Self is experienced as a destiny or "calling," and this is the quintessence of meaning or significance in life. As the hardest thing in life to explicate, it gives rise to an almost unlimited variety of symbolic expression, as we shall see in the next chapter.

The movement or transformation through which the individual goes in the process of Self-actualization [36] involves a continual synthesis of something conscious with its unconscious opposite, and is cyclic in nature, since one synthesis becomes the conscious pole of the next higher one.[37] The synthesis itself, Jung called the *transcendent function,* since it represents a knowledge that transcends the established psychological functions, albeit a transitory one. The process of a known and an unknown yielding a higher

---

[34] Arguments to justify doing this are presented in ch. 3.

[35] C. W., vol. 8, par. 45. "On Psychic Energy."

[36] The terms "self-actualization" and "psychological growth," which have become Shibboleths in contemporary American psychology, have their origin in Jung's work, although he is rarely given credit for it. The connection of these later occurrences to Jung's work is discussed in ch. 6.

[37] This is obviously similar to the thesis, antithesis, and synthesis of the Hegelian dialectic. For Jung, the dialectical process is an empirical psychological matter, and not a principle of logic or of history, as it is in Hegel's viewpoint.

27

understanding, Jung called *individuation*, since it represents the unfolding of a particular personality out of a vast field of possibilities. (Individuation is quite different from individualism, which places one-sided stress on introversion and the will to power, rather than on their synthesis with other aspects of the whole.)

The process of individuation provides us our glimpses into the unconscious, and so the relevance of the unconscious in our lives is inextricably bound up with it. To develop an admissible psychology of the process, we shall have to look into the biological possibility of such a thing; though the psyche is not reducible to it, the biological substrate is never far behind (or below). What we have covered so far has been too highly structured not to presuppose a good deal of prestructuring of the organism that exhibits it. We will have to take up that question, too.

# CHAPTER 3

# The Collective Unconscious and the Universal Forms

". . . we are not of today or of yesterday; we are of an immense age." (Interview with John Freeman of the BBC, Spring, 1959.)

I have known very few psychologists unwilling to accept the truisms that a cultural-historical perspective is essential in psychology, and that without it, one is almost sure to mistake the peculiarities of one's own culture for human universals.[1] Only by finding those cultural patterns and products that emerge again and again in different human groups can we know what is really "human nature," part of an evolutionary heritage, and neither caused nor significantly modified by the individual's life experience. Jung's concept of the *collective unconscious*, which has been so widely maligned and misrepresented, is really nothing but a working hypothesis based on such observations. I have seen no adequate discussion of the collective unconscious in any academic psychology textbook; I ask the reader to rid his mind of whatever he may have heard about it in the past, before reading on.

A particularly impressive observation, which had a formative

---

[1] Both Freud and Adler have been criticized for supposing European cultural norms of their time, such as the shrouding of sexuality in prohibition and taboo, and the high valuation of power over others, to be equally significant in all human groups. Today we witness the immense popularity of the psychologist, Maslow (see chapter 6, below), who supposes the most highly developed, "self-actualized" human character to embody the American cultural values of good "interpersonal relations," independence, and restlessly extraverted preoccupation with change and technological progress. We have not yet learned to guard against this mistake.

29

effect on Jung's thinking was of a schizophrenic Swiss man of about forty, who had delusions of being God and Christ in one person:[2]

> About 1906 I came across a very curious delusion in a paranoid schizophrenic who had been interned for many years. The patient had suffered since his youth and was incurable. He had been educated at a State school and been employed as a clerk in an office. He had no special gifts, and I myself knew nothing of mythology or archaeology in those days, so the situation was not in any way suspect. One day I found the patient standing at the window, wagging his head and blinking into the sun. He told me to do the same, for then I would see something very interesting. When I asked him what he saw, he was astonished that I could see nothing, and said: "Surely you see the sun's penis—when I move my head to and fro, it moves too, and that is where the wind comes from." Naturally I did not understand this strange idea in the least, but I made a note of it. Then about four years later during my mythological studies, I came upon a book by the late Albrecht Dieterich,[3] the well known philologist, which threw light on this fantasy. The work, published in 1910,[4] deals with a Greek papyrus in the Bibliothèque Nationale, Paris. Dieterich believed he had discovered a Mithraic ritual in one part of the text. The text is undoubtedly a religious prescription for carrying out certain incantations in which Mithras is named. It comes from the Alexandrian school of mysticism and shows affinities with certain passages in the Leiden papyri and the *Corpus Hermeticum*. In Dieterich's text we read the following directions:

> "Draw breath from the rays, draw in three times as strongly as you can and you will feel yourself raised up and walking towards the height, and you will seem to be in the middle of the aerial region. . . . The path of the visible gods will appear through the disc of the sun, who is God my father. Likewise the so-called tube, the origin of the ministering wind. For you will see hanging down from the disc of the sun something that looks like a tube. And towards the

---

[2] C. W., vol. 91, pars. 105-106. "The Concept of the Collective Unconscious."

[3] *Eine Mithrasliturgie.* Leipzig, 1903; 2nd. edn., 1910.

[4] Jung did not know about the earlier, first edition when he wrote this. The patient, however, had been hospitalized since well prior to 1903, when the first edition came out.

regions westward it is as though there were an infinite east wind. But if the other wind should prevail towards the regions of the east, you will in like manner see the vision veering in that direction." [5] It is obviously the author's intention to enable the reader to experience the vision which he had, or which at least he belicves in. The reader is to be initiated into the inner religious experience either of the author, or—what seems more likely—of one of those mystic communities of which Philo Judaeus gives contemporary accounts. The fire- or sun-god here invoked is a figure which has close historical parallels, for instance with the Christ-figure of the Apocalypse. It is therefore a 'représentation collective," as are also the ritual actions described, such as the imitating of animal noises, etc. The vision is embedded in a religious context of a distinctly ecstatic nature and describes a kind of initiation into mystic experience of the deity.

This prompted Jung, probably with some naïve idea about hereditary transmission of memory in mind, to work with uneducated American Negro mental patients in St. Elizabeths Hospital in Washington, D.C., during a trip to America in 1912.[6] He found them far more similar to Europeans in their dreams than in the waking state. There was one impressive instance of a known mythical content, a dream of a man being crucified on a turning wheel, as in the Greek myth of Ixion. The dreamer's cultural background, of course, would have called for crucifixion on a cross, and the likelihood that he had ever been exposed to the myth itself, was practically nonexistent.

A third impressive example, particularly rich in relevance to the discussion that will follow, is a case Jung treated several years later. The patient was a twenty-five year old unmarried lady who complained of excessive emotionality, a fever of 100° whenever she got emotionally excited, and a disagreeable finickiness, which made her unpleasant to deal with.[7] Her dreams early in the analysis ranged from the tiresomely prosaic, to weird erotic fantasies suggestive of latent psychosis; nothing to the point in her treatment came of them. Jung lapsed into a patronizing attitude toward her, until he had a dream of having to strain his neck to look up at

[5] Op. cit., Dieterich, p. 6.
[6] C. W., vol. 5, par. 154. Symbols of Transformation.
[7] C. W., vol. 16, pars. 546-563. "The Realities of Practical Psychotherapy."

her standing on the highest parapet of a great castle. That dream served as a corrective to his "looking down" attitude, and this improvement triggered off a series of changes in her that were completely incomprehensible at the time.

First, she experienced a vague excitation of the perineal region, and dreamed of a white elephant coming out of her vagina. This was followed by a series of very tangible psychosomatic symptoms: first in the uterus, then the bladder, and then in the gastrointestinal tract. Finally, she became troubled by the idea that her cranium was becoming soft, and that a bird with a very long, pointed beak would pierce through it, all the way down to her diaphragm. It particularly impressed Jung that she was extremely gratified by these weird experiences, while he was merely perplexed by them.

At about that time, the first thorough account of Tantaric, Kundalini Yoga appeared (*The Serpent Power* by Sir John Woodroffe, under the pseudonym of Arthur Avalon), and Jung got hold of it. Kundalini Yoga is an ontogeny of consciousness, tracing it through seven centers, or *chakras*. The first is a perineal one, containing a sacred white elephant! The second is in the bladder, the third, in the solar plexus, the fourth, in the region of the heart and diaphragm, the fifth and sixth, in the head, and the seventh, the cranium. A feminine snake, *Kundalini*, is said to wake from sleep in the first *chakra*, and ascend, activating the experiences of each level as she goes. A goddess of creation is also part of the myth.

Subsequently, the patient became interested in having a baby, a wish that seemed so prosaic and conventional to her that she wished to hide it. It later became evident that this "extraneous" thought had been symbolized by the intruding bird. When something known touched those unconscious contents, and made their synthesis with the conscious attitude possible, the personality grew enough to be able to include both rich, sensitive inner experience and a satisfying life including a husband and a child. Matters of great personal, and even somatic, significance are tied up in such universal symbols.

These observations stand out from among the vast number that Jung made, in that there was virtually no possibility they

32

could have been mere forgotten memories of things the persons who produced them had seen or heard; they were genuinely spontaneous.[8] I know of less than ten cases in Jung's work where the complete innocence of models in the production of archaic symbols was so assured. The many other observations that come without such assurances must stand only on their plausibility, which is considerable when one comes to appreciate the marvelous way that universal symbols express and became interwined with the personal lives of those who produce them in their dreams and fantasies.

Briefly stated, the hypothesis of the collective unconscious is that *there are universal symbols and myths which are a function of the nature of the psyche itself;* accordingly, they are produced by different people in different times and places, when the human situations they symbolize call them forth—or *constellate* them, as Jung would say. The collective unconscious, then is functionally distinct from the *personal unconscious,* which is the repository of forgotten personal memories.[9]

---

[8] Jung was very sensitive to the factor of early suggestions and experiences in apparently spontaneous creativity. In fact, he had originally set out to reduce as many "creative" symptoms as possible to that influence, and referred to the phenomenon as *cryptomnesia.* He discovered a particularly interesting instance of it in a passage from Nietzsche's *Thus Spake Zarathustra,* which he noticed was almost identical to a passage in *Letters from Prevorst,* an obscure book by Justinus Kerner. Jung wrote to Nietzsche's surviving sister, and learned from her that Nietzsche had indeed read Kerner's book as a child, and not remembered it as an adult. (C. W., vol. 1, pars. 140-141. *On the Psychology of So-Called Occult Phenomena.*)

[9] This way of conceiving of the unconscious was prefigured in a dream Jung had shortly before the trip to America with Freud in 1909: "I dreamed that I was in 'my home,' apparently on the first floor, in a cozy, pleasant sitting room furnished in the manner of the 18th century. I was astonished that I had never seen this room before, and began to wonder what the ground floor was like. I went downstairs and found the place was rather dark, with paneled walls and heavy furniture dating from the 16th century or even earlier. My surprise and curiosity increased. I wanted to see more of the whole structure of this house. So I went down to the cellar, where I found a door opening onto a flight of stone steps that led to a large vaulted room. The floor consisted of large slabs of stone and the walls seemed very ancient. I examined the mortar and found it was mixed with splinters of brick. Obviously the walls were of Roman origin. I became increasingly excited. In one corner, I saw an iron ring on a stone slab. I pulled up the slab and saw yet another narrow flight of steps leading to a kind of cave, which seemed to be

The universal symbols *per se*, Jung called *archetypes*. He se-
lected that term with Kant's categories in mind, which are said
to be necessarily similar from one mind to another, in order for
different persons' thoughts to agree and be communicable. Since
the psyche is thought to produce universal symbols or forms as a
result of the way it is structured, the hypothesis of the collective
unconscious has nothing to do with inherited memories or reminiscences.[10]

The archetypes are pure form. They ". . . might be compared
to the crystal lattice which is preformed in the crystalline solution.
It should not be confused with the variously structured axial
system of the individual crystal," [11] The archetype, then, represents the operation, on a different level, of the same process
that gives rise to a *Gestalt* in the Gestalt Psychology of Wertheimer, Köhler, and Koffka.[12] A perceptual or cognitive *Gestalt*
(lit. form, shape, or configuration) represents the segregation of
a perceptual or cognitive field into a figure and ground (as Edgar

---

a prehistoric tomb, containing two skulls, some bones, and broken shards of
pottery. Then I woke up." (*Man and His Symbols*, New York: Doubleday,
1964, p. 56. A similar account appears in *Memories, Dreams, and Reflections,
Op. cit.*, pp. 158-159.) This dream became a bone of contention between
Freud and Jung, since Freud emphasized the two skulls, and attributed them
to a death wish on Jung's part.

[10] This was made explicit only in Jung's later works. (See C. W., vol. 8,
par. 229, "Constitution and Heredity in Psychology," and par. 320, "The
Structure of the Psyche.") Ambiguous references to "primordial images" and
"imprints" make some of his earlier discussion vulnerable to misunderstanding, but I have not been able find the "inherited ideas" or "racial memories"
with which his critics have so often belabored him. In a letter to Bernhard
Milt, April 13, 1946, he said, "I have often asked myself whether the term
"archetype" (primordial image) is a happy one. In general I find it most
disadvantageous to let neologisms run riot in any science. The science then
becomes too specialized in an unjustifiable way and loses contact with the
world. I therefore prefer to use terms that are also current in other fields, at
the risk of provoking occasional misunderstandings." (Adler, Gerhard and
Aniela Jaffé, Eds. *C. G. Jung Letters, vol.* 1. Princeton: Princeton University
Press, 1973).

[11] C. W., vol. 8, par. 589n. "The Psychological Foundations of Belief in
Spirits."

[12] The affinity of Jung's psychology and Gestalt Psychology is treated in
detail below in chapter 6. Also, Gestalt Psychology should not be confused
with the so-called *Gestalt* psychotherapy of F. Perds, which has practically
nothing to do with its older namesake.

Rubin put it), according to certain psychological laws. The meaningful whole so produced is different from, and not reducible to, its constituent parts. Consequently, one cannot learn its nature by reductive study of the parts. Since this organization is consistent and lawful, and only to a limited extent modifiable by learning, both Jung's psychology and Gestalt Psychology place particular emphasis on inborn, "native" factors.

This emphasis on native factors is precisely the reason why Jung's psychology has received so little acceptance in academic psychology circles, where the principal emphasis has been on those aspects of behavior extensively modifiable by learning. Ever since Pavlov discovered the conditioned reflex in Russia, and E. L. Thorndike formulated the laws of learning in America, psychologists have studied the learning of lower animals in artificial situations, expecting to gain an understanding of the human psyche from that. These same researchers have usually had little knowledge of, or appreciation for, the inflexible, species-specific behaviors that account for almost all of any infra-human animal's adaptation to its natural environment, or for the helplessness and passivity of adaptation of animals in captivity.

Such a one-sidedly learning-oriented approach naturally finds only a superficial application to the human condition, and today we witness a reaction to it in the form of a renewed emphasis on instinct. On Aggression, by the German ethologist Konrad Lorenz, The Naked Ape by Desmond Morris, The Territorial Imperative by Robert Ardrey, and The Imperial Animal by Lionel Tiger and Robin Fox, have made the direct comparison of human social behavior to automatic, species-specific animal adaptations a fashionable intellectual pastime. The two approaches share the error of equating human and infra-human behavior, which are qualitatively differentiated by man's profoundly greater flexibility and his ability to symbolize and reflect.

From the proposition that man is more than a mere creature of instinct; it does not follow that he comes into the world with just a tabula rasa. He comes into the world equipped to structure and give meaning to the evidence of his senses. The archetype is an essential part of that equipment, and resolves the dilemma of the two views: we exchange our dichotomy between learned and innate factors for one between man acting blindly out of instinct, and man detached from his immediate surroundings, able to put the past and the possibilities of a thing into perspective, i.e., able to reflect.

> Archetype and instinct are the most polar opposites imaginable, as can easily be seen when one compares a man who is ruled by his instinctual drives with a man who is seized by the spirit. But just as between all opposites there obtains so close a bond that no position can be established or even thought of without its corresponding negation, so in this case also "les extrêmes se touchent." They belong together as correspondences, which is not to say that the one is derivable from the other, but that they subsist side by side as reflections in our own minds of the opposition that underlies all psychic energy. Man finds himself simultaneously driven to act and free to reflect. This contrariety in his nature has no moral significance, for instinct is not in itself bad any more than spirit is good. Both can be both.[13]

Just as a nativistic standpoint evokes a prejudice in psychological circles, arising from ideological rather than empirical considerations, teleological standpoints evoke one in biological circles. Since the question of the possibility, from a biological standpoint, of a person growing toward a goal that transcends his mere conscious intentions (individuation), and prefiguring the goal in symbolic expression, will inevitably arise, we must deal with it.

Naturphilosophie, the precursor of modern biology, was highly teleological. The concept of the scala naturae, or a rational ordering of living species from the lowest to the highest inherent in nature, pervades early biological work. Interestingly, the Naturphilosophen used the term, "archetype" to denote inherent patterns that life existed to realize.[14] With positivism and reductionism, biology has gravitated to the opposite one-sided extreme, in the form of the synthetic theory of evolution.[15]

According to the synthetic theory of evolution, the origin of the species is entirely a causal matter. Random genetic mutations

---

[13] C. W., vol. 8, par. 406. "On the Nature of the Psyche."

[14] Koestler, Arthur. The Ghost in the Machine. New York: Macmillan, 1967, pp. 137-140.

[15] Simpson, G. G. "The Study of Evolution: Methods and Present Status of Theory." In: Simpson, G. G., and Roe, A., eds. Behavior and Evolution. New Haven: Yale U. Press, 1958.

(changes of the genotype) produce changes in the structure and behavior (phenotype) of the organism. The overwhelming majority of such alterations undermine a strain's adaptation, and put it at a propagatory disadvantage. A very few such changes will happen to improve its adaptation, and cause the characteristic involved to be preserved and spread because the strain makes a better showing in the competition for survival. This is the famous Darwinian process of natural selection. This process, of course, can account only for the evolution of characteristics that directly influence the propagation of a species from generation to generation.

There are many things one can observe in nature that place intolerable strain on the synthetic theory. Firstly, one would expect the structures that evolve to show a variety comparable to the variety of adaptations needing to be made. While a superficial look at the variety of species may seem to verify that expectation, a systematic analysis reveals a few basic patterns or designs, of which there are many variations or homologues.[16] For example, the forefin of a whale, the wing of a bird, the forefoot of a quadruped, and the hand of a man are all homologous variations of one characteristic design. The same holds true for different species. Consider the way forelimbs evolved into wings in prehistoric flying reptiles, and did so again in the evolution of modern birds. In Australia, there are mice, flying squirrels, and wolves which are marsupials, in which the gestation of young takes place without a placenta, and the young are carried and nursed in a pouch on the mother's body. Their evolution must have taken place in complete isolation from that of the corresponding placental animals, and yet, the parallelness of design is startling. It gives a certain credence to the "archetypes" of the Naturphilosophen!

More importantly, organisms show all kinds of resources for new adaptations without needing to wait for the right mutation, or for the debacle of all the other, wrong mutations.[17] A few years ago, blue tits started to pierce milk bottle caps with their beaks, and inside a single season, were doing so all over Europe. I recall hearing stories in East Africa of elephants which, when one of

---

[16] See Koestler, Op. cit., pp. 127-150.
[17] Ibid., pp. 151-171.

their herd had been shot by an ivory hunter, would stay with him until he died, pull out his tusks, and break them to pieces. This could serve no conceivable purpose, except to thwart the ivory hunters. The ultimate example is, of course, man's intelligence. Not much natural selection can have taken place since man learned to write, to make music, to fly, and to split the atom. The synthetic theory of evolution cannot account for the appearance of such capabilities, which must have been present many times longer than they have been in use. To stick to an explanation that cannot account for the facts is not scientific; it is better to keep an open mind to the possibility of universal forms in nature, and a teleological process at work, if that seems to account for the facts.

\*    \*    \*

We have already implied that archetypes give structure to symbols, which express the life situation of the person who produces them, and prefigure the individuation of his particular personality out of the background of possibilities represented by his collective unconscious. Since the "normal" process is a continual assimilation of unconscious contents to the conscious attitude, so that it becomes more differentiated and better able to call upon the energetic resources of the unconscious areas of the individual psyche, it follows that a Jungian analysis is intended to aid the process, and that a person who would seek a Jungian as a therapist would be as likely merely to be aware of a certain psychological stagnation in himself, as to suffer from some discrete neurotic symptom. (The ambiguity of the therapeutic task leads to a multitude of pitfalls, which we shall cover in chapter 7.)

If there is any one invariable law governing the dreams, fantasies, and spontaneous artistic endeavors that provide the material for a Jungian analysis, it is that they are compensatory to the conscious attitude. They supply something that is needed for understanding, that psychological opposite with its own element of truth to contribute. If the conscious attitude becomes too one-sided and rigidified, then the corrective is not assimilated: instead, it becomes an autonomous complex that will assert itself against the conscious personality, as described in the first chapter, above. Instead of the ongoing integration of the personality which is individuation, a division of the personality against itself takes place.[18]

The technique of Jungian analysis is particularly flexible; a few generalizations can be made about it, nevertheless. The free association of the Freudian method, being extremely inefficient and tedious, is seldom used. Great attention is paid to dreams. Since it is seldom possible to be sure what a single dream means, series of dreams, and trends noted in them, are needed for the analysis to proceed. While literary and mythological background is indispensable in bringing the needed insight and synthesis about, the relationship of the dream to the dreamer is paramount and must take precedence over mere intellectual comparison of the dream to its historical antecedents: "Learn as much as you can about symbolism; then forget it all when you are analyzing a dream." [19] The ultimate criterion for an interpretation is the satisfaction of the person to whom it pertains. If it "rings true" for him, then it has value. Thus, more than one interpretation may be fruitful.

If there is any receptivity to the dark side of the Ego at all, conscious fantasy may be used to fill in the gaps in dreams. Allowing the needed material to emerge is referred to as *active imagination*. When the process is helped along by a few discreet questions from the therapist, it is called *amplification*.[20] The same receptivity that makes active imagination possible, if better developed, can also yield up whole fantasies and artistic creations,

---

[18] This formulation of neurosis, it should be noted, does not contradict the conventional Freudian one; rather, it is more comprehensive. It handles those dissociations which are not guilt-toned enough to be called repressions, where a certain distortion of the Freudian model is needed for it to accomodate them.

[19] *Man and His Symbols, Op. cit.,* p. 56.

[20] This obviously opens up the possibility that the suggestions of the therapist may be mistaken for authentic insights. Jung minimized this danger, as he thought that a person would always reject a spurious interpretation in the end. Such manipulation can, at least, be worse than no therapy at all, since, by increasing the alienation of the conscious attitude from the unconscious, it makes the neurosis worse. This is taken up further in chapter 7.

which can be interpreted just like dreams. The interpretation of pictures drawn by the patient is frequently done.[21]

The therapist and the patient meet on as equal terms as possible in therapy, so the typical posture is face to face. This makes for an honest encounter between real people, rather than the transference that the Freudians so insist upon.[22] Since childhood conflicts are not an essential issue in every case, a transference is not always necessary or even desirable. When it does occur, it may take on a much different significance than in other types of therapy, as we shall see.

Respect for the patient as ethically free and independent is a much more central reason for an egalitarian approach to therapy. Unless the patient was clearly incompetent or dangerous, Jung eschewed controlling him or fostering more dependency than necessary. For that reason, he gave up hypnosis very early, and probably would not have approved of the indiscriminate use of tranquilizing and anti-depressant drugs so common in psychiatry nowadays.

The ethical problem, and the problem of good and evil it presupposes, is encountered very early in one's personal coming to terms with the unconscious; that is why the Freudians saw it as the entirety of the problem. Since most people have their best foot forward most of the time, the evil in them is relatively unconscious. Our inferior, negative aspect is consistently found as a complex, symbolized or personified as a sinister person in our dreams; it is so consistent that we must also call it an archetype. Jung called it the *shadow*, since it is a polar opposite to the light of consciousness, and the brighter the light, the more distinct the shadow. This imago represents the opposite, the negation of all our good intentions; its interference with what we try to do is symptomatic.[23]

---

[21] Jung, himself, liked to chisel his fantasy into stone, and became quite a competent sculptor in his later years.

[22] Transference is the recapitulation in therapy of early relationships with parents and significant others, with the therapist in the role of the other.

[23] Most Americans are familiar with the Yiddish world *schlemiel*, which refers to a person whose conscious intentions are chronically backfiring, we would say because of the autonomy of the shadow. There is also a Swiss-German expression for it, *Pechvögel* ("pitch-bird").

Since the shadow may be personified as a member of a different race or some other out-group, the projection of the shadow accounts for a great deal of prejudice and outgroup hostility. The evil we see in them is really unconscious in us. In the extreme case, projection of the shadow is manifested as delusions of persecution. When one considers that delusions of grandeur—an extreme kind of inflation—are the result of too close an identification with some unconscious archetype, or with the persona, making the shadow more unconscious and more apt to be projected than it would otherwise be, it then becames easy to see why delusions of persecution and of grandeur find such an affinity for one another in paranoia.

A particularly fine illustration of the reciprocal relationship between the conscious personality and the shadow is the movie, *The French Connection* (thanks to some inspired liberties with the original story taken by the script writers).[24] The protagonist is a New York City narcotics policeman, who is vulgar, brutal, ruthless, and disorganized. The villain whom he pursues is a French narcotics smuggler, whose unconscious origins are symbolized by his coming from across the ocean, and speaking another language. He is complete with a symbol of the libido he has brought with him, i.e. the load of heroin he brings in concealed in the rocker panels of a Lincoln Continental. He is urbane, civilized, honorable in his own way, and superbly well organized: the perfect opposite of the hero. Like every man's shadow, he eludes capture and makes it back across the water, albeit depotentiated for the time being by the capture of the heroin.

*The Picture of Dorian Gray*, by Oscar Wilde, and *The Strange Case of Dr. Jekyll and Mr. Hyde*, by Robert Louis Stevenson are examples of the shadow in literature. We encounter an impersonal

---

[24] There is also, unfortunately, a great deal of contrived, unauthentic use of Jungian symbols in movies and other American popular culture, probably because there are many writers and artists among the patients of the Jungian analysts of New York and Los Angeles. Recently I went to see one escapist movie (*J. W. Coop*) which includes a scene where the heroine is lying in bed reading a paperback copy of *Man and His Symbols* as the hero returns from the forced landing of a light plane he has been flying. I suppose that is the ultimate "in joke."

form of the shadow in the Christian devil. The myth of Satan having originally been in God's presence, but having been cast out of heaven when the world was created, parallels differentiation of the shadow when the individual comes to consciousness.

Since the personal shadow compensates for the conscious attitude, a person who is manifestly bad will have a good shadow that may trip him up in realizing his bad intentions. Nietzsche's pale felon, and Shakespeare's Falstaff are such characters.

The careful reader should, at this point, be a little confused that the shadow is not the bridge to the unconscious we have earlier claimed the dark side of the Ego, on one level, and the inferior function, on another, to be. That bridge is provided by a more comprehensive entity, the *soul*.

The soul is the entire dark, semi-conscious side of the Ego, and is reciprocal to the persona, at least in the usual case where the conscious personality is heavily identified with the persona. It is the least conscious aspect of one's experience that can be identified as one's own. Being so closely associated with unconsciousness, it is the locus of conscious experience of the process of individuation taking place; this makes it the cherished essence of one's being. In the lore of primitive peoples, and also in the work of many western writers, the phenomenon of loss of the soul is referred to, and that is a state of meaninglessness and stagnation. Jung describes the phenomenon, which he experienced during the "fallow" period between the break with Freud, and the beginning of major work on his own ideas:

> . . . I had written down a fantasy of my soul having flown away from me. This was a significant event: the soul . . . establishes the relationship to the unconscious. In a certain sense this is also a relationship to the collectivity of the dead: for the unconscious corresponds to the mythic land of the dead, the land of the ancestors. If, therefore, one has a fantasy of the soul vanishing, this means that it has withdrawn into the unconscious or into the land of the dead. There it produces a mysterious animation and gives visible form to the ancestral traces, the collective contents. Like a medium, it gives the dead a chance to manifest themselves.[25]

---

[25] *Op. cit.*, *Memories, Dreams, Reflections*, p. 191.

The soul exists, then, in contrast to unconscious contents which are also experienced, but not as part of oneself, and these are known as *spirits*. In structural terms, a spirit is comparable to an autonomous complex, which may also be an archetype, if it takes a general or universal form. The spirit is said to enter a person ("I don't know what got into me, what possessed me." "I'll do it when the spirit moves me."), or the person may call upon it ("I shall ask God to give me strength, insight, etc." "I shall call upon the muse."). Whether the spirit answers, of course, is not under conscious control. When one is creative, one says that ideas occur *to* one. Many writers of fiction describe how they do not control the characters they create, and Thomas Mann even described his books as having written themselves. The distinction between soul and spirit is not inherent in the imagos themselves, but depends on the relationship of consciousness to them. As their affinity to consciousness increases, it is hard to tell where spirit experience leaves off, and soul experience begins. Jung summed up the essence of the difference: ". . . primitive pathology recognizes two causes of illness: loss of soul, and possession by a spirit."[26]

The experience of the soul is greatly affected by the universal opposites of masculine and feminine.[27] Since the soul is reciprocal to the persona, it is experienced, personified, and projected as being of the opposite sex.[28] Jung used the term *anima* (Latin for "soul") for the masculine soul experience, and *animus* (Latin

---

[26] C. W., vol. 8, par. 587. "The Psychological Foundations of Belief in Spirits."

[27] When I present these ideas in my university classes, I encounter bitter opposition from the women's liberationists, who take the extraverted view that masculinity and femininity are a superficial effect of social indoctrination. The relevance of Jung's psychology to women's problems is taken up in chapter 5.

[28] Except in homosexuality, where the Ego is most strongly identified with the soul, leaving the persona out of consciousness so that it is projected. (C. W., vol. 6, par. 809, *Psychological Types*.) The witty, catty, creative intelligence that one often notices in homosexuals and effeminate men is due to a special closeness to the unconscious. In a sense, the superior completeness that some homosexuals claim to experience, is justified.

43

for "spirit"!) for the corresponding feminine one.[29] Since the inferior function, the least differentiated aspect of one's own personality (slowly emerging in individuation) is represented in these soul-images, it is the content of the projection of them.

Falling in love, being wildly infatuated with another person, is one result of such a soul projection. (Here we must differentiate the mystery of love from mere falling in love: if there were no such distinction, the coming of the projected content to consciousness, and the resulting withdrawal of the projection, would always bring an end to love. Fortunately, experience does not show this to be the case.) By falling in love, the lover tries to compensate for his weak side by an easier means than developing it, and places himself in danger of falling in love with his own worst weaknesses:

> If you take a typical intellectual who is terribly afraid of falling in love, you will think his fear very foolish. But he is most probably right, because he will very likely make foolish nonsense when he falls in love. He will be caught most certainly, because his feeling only reacts to an archaic or to a dangerous kind of woman. This is why many intellectuals are inclined to marry beneath them. They are caught by the landlady perhaps, or by the cook, because they are unaware of their archaic feeling through which they get caught. But they are right to be afraid . . . in their feelings they can be influenced . . . they can be cheated, and they know it. Therefore never force a man into his feeling when he is an intellectual. He controls it with an iron hand because it is very dangerous.[30]

The compensatory function of the soul-image also manifests itself in dreams, where the anima or animus figure often provides some insight needed to round out a too onesided conscious attitude. Many examples could be given; to express the point, I hope it will be sufficient to give one typical one, a dream of young lady who knew nothing of Jung's psychology. At the time, a very desirable young man wanted to marry her, but some inner resist-

---

[29] In their original usages, the terms "spirit" and "soul" are intertwined with the Greek concept of pneuma, where wind or breath is the semi-material entity that gives life of the material body of a living being.
[30] Op. cit., Analytical Psychology . . ., p. 20.

ance for which she could not account stopped her from accepting his proposal. She dreamed she was in a board-of-directors room atop a skyscraper, seated at one end of a long table, the young man at the other end. All along the sides of the table were seated human-sized rabbits, collectively representing her animus [31] (she had been reading a children's book, in which the characters were rabbits, that day). They were telling her she must not marry him, because she did not love him. After that, she decided to refuse his offer, and remained content thereafter that that was the right decision.

If there is any one pivotal aspect of the masculine soul experience, the anima (and therefore of feminine psychology) it is Eros, the feeling relationship to other people. Since that is the inferior part of the masculine psychology, needing to be integrated for there to be a higher consciousness, a man must learn of it from his anima. The literary examples of such anima tutelage are legion: Dante's Beatrice, and Goethe's apparition of Helen of Troy in Faust, are classical examples. Hermine in Hesse's Steppenwolf is a particularly good modern example, and Jung particularly liked She by H. Rider Haggard, and Atlantida by Pierre Benoît, as examples. Most men experience it in the magical fascination exerted by a fairy-like, vacantly beautiful woman, of which Garbo is a good example. A section of Edgar Allen Poe's "To Helen" [32] captures the essence, if perhaps a little too intensely for contemporary tastes:

> All—all expired save thee—save less than thou:
> Save only the divine light in thine eyes—
> Save but the soul in thine uplifted eyes.
> I saw but them—they were the world to me.
> I saw but them—saw only them for hours—
> Saw only them until the moon went down.
> What wild heart-histories seemed to lie enwritten
> Upon those crystalline, celestial spheres!
> How dark a woe! yet how sublime a hope!
> How silently serene a sea of pride!
> How daring an ambition! yet how deep—
> How fathomless a capacity for love!

---

[31] The animus frequently takes the plural form, while the anima seldom does so. The reasons for this are taken up shortly, below.

[32] The later of two poems by that name published by him.

45

The rôle of the anima in individuation is epitomized in two works of Ludwig von Beethoven. (Jung, who was unmusical, did not take them up, as far as I know.) Beethoven's only opera, *Fidelio*, is a pure allegory of the realization of the Self. I was charmed by it long before I became interested in Jungian psychology, and could not understand why, since the story was so manifestly silly, and had overtones of homosexuality that were a little offensive to my up-tight southern mentality.

*Fidelio* takes place in a prison somewhere in Spain in the eighteenth century. Florestan, a nobleman, is held in the darkest subterranean dungeon there, as a political prisoner (the condition of the Self in the unindividuated person). His wife Leonora, in order to confirm his whereabouts and gain his release, has disguised herself as a boy, and secured employment as an attendant in the prison, which is superintended by the dependable, loyal, rather passive jailmaster, Rocco. Rocco's daughter, Marcellina, falls in love with the new attendant, known to them only as "Fidelio," and therefore gives the air to the gatekeeper, Jaquino, who had been courting her. "Fidelio" must play along with Marcellina, to avoid blowing her cover.

One day Don Pizarro, the evil absentee governor of the prison, who has vengefully imprisoned Florestan, unbeknown to the latter's friends (who think him dead) and the former's superiors, comes to the prison in a high dudgeon. He finds Rocco exercising the prisoners from the upper, semi-dark dungeons against orders, and is angry. Rocco uses his best diplomacy to calm him down. Next we learn that Pizarro has been warned of a surprise inspection by Don Fernando, the Minister of State. Pizarro tells how he must murder Florestan immediately, so that the minister will not find him there; he gives Rocco some extra money to go down to the lowest dungeon and dig a grave for Florestan, whom Pizarro will come down later to murder. After some lame protest, Rocco agrees. Up to this point, Rocco has allowed no one but himself to attend the dark dungeon, because he does not wish to subject "Fidelio" to the dreadful sight of the prisoner whom, under orders from Pizarro, he is systematically starving.

Needing help to open the cistern in which the grave is to be dug, he allows "Fidelio" to accompany him down into the dungeon. Florestan lies in chains, asleep, as the two enter with a lantern. He awakes, and a conversation ensues. Rocco declares he would like to help his prisoner, but to do so would be futile, and only place himself in jeopardy. Florestan notices the similarity between "Fidelio" and Leonora, and thinks it a delusion brought on by his starved condition. Pizarro comes with his knife and is about to strike, when "Fidelio" produces a pistol and holds him at bay; at almost the same moment a bugle blows, heralding the arrival of the minister. Just then, Rocco decides he can obey the tyrant no longer, and all go to the surface to meet the governor, and turn Pizarro in.

The last scene, in the courtyard on the surface, is more like a cantata than an act of an opera. A chorus, ostensibly made up of guards and townspeople, is arranged in a three-sided square, and the minister stands in the center with all the protagonists arranged around him. The minister announces that he has come to end tyranny, and foster brotherly love. He directs Rocco to unchain Florestan, but then alters the direction, and Leonora is given the key so she might do it, since she alone is qualified for that honor. The music and libretto emphasize the ecstasy of the moment of liberation, and the final choruses praise the triumph of God's justice and brotherly love, possible through the wife who rescues her husband.

So the shadow (Pizarro) is confronted, and robbed of his power (depotentiated through insight, so that he is reflected about rather than acted out.) The spirit of justice, who is universal and impersonal, can then be called upon. The anima can be revealed, and bring about a synthesis of opposites (of which the most obvious ones in this example are good and evil) which is an ecstatic experience, an experience of transformation. That the relationship of Leonora to the transformation awed Beethoven is shown in his having written four versions of the Leonora Overture that goes with the opera, and never having been able to synthesize them into one, ultimate Leonora Overture. The same preoccupations are seen in the Choral (Ninth) Symphony, for which Schiller's "Ode to Joy" provided the libretto. There, a "daughter of Elysium" is the key to the eruption of truth, justice, and brotherly love expressed by the work. There are many other sym-

47

bols of individuation in the foregoing, to which we shall return after completing our discussion of the soul.

To be sure, the anima also has her negative aspect, as she must, overlapping to a certain extent with the shadow. The morose moods a man is apt to fall into are examples of harmful anima influence. When one must get up in the morning, but doesn't feel like it, it is the inferior woman in one that does the whining, complaining, and feeling sorry for oneself. It usually seems very strange and far away by the second cup of coffee.

The anima can also be an accessory to the fact of inflation. Jung described the experience:

> What the anima said seemed to me full of a deep cunning. . . . She might then have easily seduced me into believing that I was a misunderstood artist, and that my so-called artistic nature gave me the right to neglect reality. If I had followed her voice, she would in all probability have said to me one day, "Do you imagine the nonsense you're engaged in is really art? Not a bit." Thus the insinuations of the anima, the mouthpiece of the unconscious, can utterly destroy a man. In the final analysis the decisive factor is always consciousness, which can understand the manifestations of the unconscious and take up a position toward them.[33]

Where the anima represents the inferior Eros in a man, the animus represents the inferior *Logos* ("discrimination, judgment, insight" [34]) in a woman. Where the anima experience is one of inspiration, or at least of sentimentality, the animus experience, at its best, is one of profundity, and ordinarily, opinionatedness. In a nutshell, "as the anima produces *moods*, so the animus produces *opinions*; and as the moods of a man issue from a shadowy background, so the opinions of a woman rest on equally unconscious prior assumptions [italics in original]." [35]

---

[33] *Op. cit., Memories, Dreams, Reflections*, p. 187.
[34] C. W., vol. 14, par. 224. *Mysterium Conunctionis.*
[35] C. W., vol. 7, par. 331. *The Relations Between the Ego and the Unconscious: Two.*

Emma Jung [36] describes the animus experience:

> The most characteristic manifestation of the animus is not
> in a configured image . . . but rather in words (*logos* also
> means word). It comes to us as a voice commenting on every
> situation in which we find ourselves, or imparting generally
> applicable rules of behavior. Often this is how we first per-
> ceive the animus to be different from the ego, long before it
> has crystalized into a personal figure. As far as I have ob-
> served, this voice expresses itself chiefly in two ways. First,
> we hear from it a critical, usually negative comment on every
> monument, an exact examination of all motives and intentions,
> which naturally always causes feeling of inferiority, and tends
> to nip in the bud all initiative and every wish for self-expres-
> sion. From time to time, this same voice may also dispense
> exaggerated praise, and the result of these extremes of judg-
> ment is that one oscillates to and fro between the conscious-
> ness of complete futility and a blown-up sense of one's own
> value and importance. This animus' second way of speaking
> is confined more or less exclusively to issuing commands or
> prohibitions, and pronouncing generally accepted view-
> points. [37]

The reader may here accuse me of hiding behind Mrs. Jung's
skirts, for using her words to illustrate the prominent, troublesome aspect of the animus. To bring this into perspective, we
must consider the feminine consciousness that supplies the
animus with its context:

> The feminine consciousness has a lunar rather than a solar
> character. Its light is the "mild" light of the moon, which
> merges things together rather than separates them. It does
> not show up objects in all their pitiless discreteness and
> separateness, like the harsh, glaring light of day, but blends
> in a deceptive shimmer the near and the far, magically trans-
> forming little things into big things, high into low, softening

---

[36] (1882-1955; née Rauschenbach) Mrs. Jung took up her husband's psychology quite earnestly in her later years, after their children were grown. In
addition to *Animus and Anima*, she undertook an extensive work, *The Grail
Legend*, but died before completing it; it was completed by Marie-Louise von
Franz (New York: C. G. Jung Foundation, 1971).

[37] *Animus and Anima*. New York: The Analytical Psychology Club, 1957,
p. 20.

all colour into a bluish haze, and blending the nocturnal landscape into unsuspected unity.[38]

Such is the conscious attitude dominated by Eros: it seeks to humanize things and situations, and make them attractive. It is introverted, and seeks to make things into a continuous, unitary whole. Therefore, the animus is extraverted, analytic, and pluralistic.[39] Accordingly, the animus often is personified in the plural, and (in contrast to the dream of the rabbits) as several characters disagreeing.

The feminine consciousness, being less intense than the masculine, allows the animus more autonomy—hence it is more like a spirit than the anima. This makes for an acute danger of animus possession. One finds it in the aggressive, professional career woman who is "just a man's mind with wings underneath, and the whole woman's body is nonexistent." [40] A professional, career-oriented woman need not always succumb to the arbitrariness and dogmatism of her animus, but she *does* need to develop a special insight in order to avoid it. There are any number of modern plays and stories where the plot revolves around a girl with a special talent that cries out to be developed into a career, and who must decide whether to give up the great love of her life for it. In contrast to the great love (usually the hero) is an impresario, mentor, etc. who urges her on, and any number of others pushing her in different directions. (To be sure, there are many myths where a male character forswears love as a precondition of some special power; the opposition of love and power is universal!)

The same lesser intensity of feminine consciousness can also make for a greater receptivity to the creative resources (spirits) of the unconscious:

> Finally . . . the animus is the incarnation of meaning . . . he becomes (like the anima) a mediator of the religious

---

[38] C. W., vol. 14, par. 223. *Mysterium Coniunctionis.*

[39] It was possible to observe the normally unconscious introversion of men and extraversion of women in schizophrenic mental patients, in the days before it became customary to keep them full of tranquillizers and anti-depressants. The men's wards were usually so quiet, one could hear a pin drop (most were diagnosed "catatonic"). The women's wards were a virtual twenty-four hour Mardi-Gras, full of noise and confusion (most were diagnosed "simple" or "hebephrenic").

[40] *Op. cit., Analytical Psychology . . .*, p. 165.

experience whereby life acquires new meaning. He gives the woman spiritual firmness, an invisible support that compensates for her outer softness. The animus in his most developed form sometimes connects the woman's mind with the spiritual evolution of her age, and can thereby make her even more receptive than a man to new creative ideas. It is for this reason that in earlier times women were used by many nations as diviners and seers. The creative boldness of their positive animus at times expresses thoughts and ideas that stimulate men to new enterprises.[41]

The rôle of the animus in individuation is exemplified in the following vision, produced with active imagination by one of Jung's woman patients:

> I climbed the mountain and came to a place where I saw seven red stones in front of me, seven on either side, and seven behind me. I stood in the middle of this quadrangle. The stones were flat like steps. I tried to lift the four stones nearest me. In doing so I discovered that these stones were the pedestals of four statues of gods buried upside down in the earth. I dug them up and arranged them about me so I was standing in the middle of them. Suddenly they leaned towards one another until their heads touched, forming something like a tent over me. I myself fell to the ground and said, "Fall upon me if you must! I am tired." Then I saw that beyond, encircling the four gods, a ring of flame had formed. After a time I got up from the ground and overthrew the statues of the gods. Where they fell, four trees shot up. At that blue flames leapt up from the ring of fire and began to burn the foliage of the trees. Seeing this I said, "This must stop. I must go into the fire myself so that the leaves shall not be burned." Then I stepped into the fire. The trees vanished and the fiery ring drew together to one immense blue flame that carried me up from the earth [italics in original].[42]

The fourfoldness of the animus is but one of countless examples of the significance of the number, four, as a symbol of individuation. Jung noticed it so often that he came to think of

---

[41] von Franz, M.-L. "The Process of Individuation." In: *Op. cit., Man and His Symbols*, pp. 194-195.

[42] C. W., vol. 7, par. 366. *The Relations between the Ego and the Unconscious: Two.*

it as a real analogue of the differentiation of the four functions. The four statues literally point to the merging of the four into one: the insolubility of the paradox of that being conceivable as a goal, but impossible for a mortal to achieve, accounts for the intense, stressed quality of the vision. It is the same problem that is symbolized by the old conundrum of squaring the circle. (The number three, accordingly, is equally ubiquitous, denoting the human condition wherein the fourth, inferior function is undifferentiated, leaving behind the awareness of three.) The conspicuous stage direction in *Fidelio*, surrounding the protagonists with a chorus forming three sides of a square during the ecstatic scene of the liberation of the Self, is another example. It is characteristic that in the masculine fantasy *Fidelio* represents, there is only one anima (Jaquino and Marcellina representing the auxiliary functions, and Rocco and Florestan, two aspects of the same thing—Beethoven's personality); instead of coming up with four animas, Beethoven came up with four Leonora Overtures that he could not merge into one.

The circle, or ring, (made up in this case of a blue fire that transforms but does not consume) is another universal symbol of individuation; such circles are most often quadrantally arranged. They also appear often as liquid-containing vessels. Jung called such a circle a *mandala* (Sandskrit for "magic circle"), and it represents a containment or "getting it together" of the personality.[43] Conversely, psychotic or nearly psychotic people will often produce the symbol of a broken circle or vessel, indicating the fragmentation of the conscious personality, and its loss of differentiation from its collective unconscious context. Using the mandala as a model, Jung came to think of individuation as a circumambulation of a center (the unattainable Self), which is another way of expressing the synthesis and resynthesis of something conscious with something unconscious we described earlier. Accordingly: "The . . . mandala is always an inner image, which is gradually built up through (active) imagination, at such times

[43] Examples with pictures may be found in C. W., vol 9 ¹, pars. 627-712, "Concerning Mandala Symbolism"; vol. 12, pars. 122-331, *Psychology and Alchemy*, 2nd. ed., and vol. 13, pars. 1-84, "Commentary on 'The Secret of the Golden Flower.'"

when psychic equilibrium is disturbed or when a thought cannot be found and must be sought for. . . ."[44]

The statues dug out of the ground are certainly "a thought [that] cannot be found and must be sought for." Their being upside down in the ground, similar to a reflection of an object in a pool of water, shows the reciprocal relationship of the conscious attitude and unconsciousness. The seven stones are stages of the coming of a secret to consciousness; the number, seven, is a universal symbol, found in such things as the seven seals, seven veils, seven chakras, etc.

\*　　\*　　\*

The process of individuation is normally gradual, and the practical-minded reader may, at this point, be on the verge of dismissing it as a mere romantic fantasy, incapable of being satisfactorily demonstrated to take place, and even if it could be, irrelevant to the practical, this-worldly concerns of most people's lives. Even Jung thought it was not something a person in the first half of life (say, under thirty-five) should normally be concerned with, since that is a time for making a place in the world, for solving economic problems, for coping with small children, etc. Spiritual development, he thought, was pertinent to later life, when the refining and differentiating course of individuation had advanced far enough to be concerned with finer nuances.[45]

There are a few extreme pathological cases that afford us an opportunity to observe individuation taking place, and to verify a transformation of the personality through the synthesis of opposites after a very short time. These are cases where the estrangement of consciousness from the unconscious is particularly acute. Two of the three examples we shall take up are from

---

[44] C. W., vol. 12, par. 123. *Psychology and Alchemy*, 2nd. ed.

[45] Jung himself had a very productive old age, continuing to do increasingly advanced and refined work even as he became physically old and feeble. His stress on completeness rather than senility as the culmination of a human life was consistent with his personal experience. There are many others who seem to reach the peak of their personal destiny early in life, and have discontented, anticlimactic existences thereafter; in this context, we would say that is because the necessary preparation for spiritual development in the second half of life has not taken place.

well known books: *The Three Faces of Eve*,[46] which was adapted reasonably accurately into a movie starring Joanne Woodward, and *I Never Promised You a Rose Garden*,[47] which has nothing to do with the popular song by that name. Both cases have (for us) the advantage of having been treated and recorded without Jungian influence; the Jungian concepts they exemplify cannot be thought to have been insinuated into them for mendacious reasons. (The authors of *The Three Faces* . . . even tried to anticipate what a Jungian would have had to say about the case,[48] and thereby established for us that they understood too little of Jung's psychology for it to have had any bearing on their actions.) The third case is a former student of mine, who was floored by the parallelness of her earlier experiences and Jung's *The Psychology of the Transference*.[49]

*The Three Faces of Eve* deals with a young, married woman with a small daughter, who consulted with the psychiatrist Thigpen, complaining of headaches, for which no physiological cause could be found. The woman (named Eve White for the purposes of the book) was a demure, dutiful, frigid housewife, in very average circumstances. In the course of psychiatric interviews, Thigpen was stunned to witness the emergence of a second personality, endowed with complete awareness of the first, and more or less opposite to it: lively, irresponsible, impulsive, and flirtatious (merely flirtatious, since she was also frigid; she exploited and teased men). It was typical of the second personality, dubbed Eve Black, to go partying and leave Eve White to have the hangover. Eve White took the news of Eve Black's existence with equanimity, almost with *belle indifférence*. It accounted for the mysterious appearance of fancy dresses in her closet, and bills for them in her husband's mail. Eve Black also had an allergy to

---

[46] Thigpen, Corbett H., and Cleckley, Hervey M. New York: Popular Library, 1957.

[47] Green, Hannah. New York: Holt, Rinehart, and Winston, 1964. This is a mildly fictionalized, first person account. A former student of mine, who had been a psychotic patient at Chestnut Lodge Hospital in Maryland, informs me that the case was treated there, and the psychiatrist, identified as "Dr. Fried" in the book, was Frieda Fromm-Reichmann.

[48] *Op. cit., The Three Faces* . . ., p. 211.

[49] C. W., vol. 16, pars. 353-539.

nylon that Eve White did not have, and so normally went bare-legged.

By means of more interviews and hypnotic regression, it was established that Eve Black had existed since age four or five, and coincided with two traumatic experiences that must have accounted for much of Eve White's constrained timorousness. These were seeing a dead man dredged up from a nearby swamp, and being forced by her mother to touch the cold face of her dead grandmother at her funeral. Twin sisters were born shortly after, and must have represented a prototype, reinforcing the pattern of dissociation. Eve Black stayed dormant during most of Eve White's schooling, since she found school boring.

Fairly early in the treatment, she had the following dream (one of only three dream sequences reported):

> I am in a tremendous room. . . . Its outline seems vague and dim because of its size. Toward the center of this room is a pool of stagnant green water. On the edge of the pool stand my husband and my uncle. I am in the water with Bonnie [her daughter]. I am trying to get her out for we both seem to be drowning, but I must not take her out where she will be near my husband or my uncle. Despite all I can do the contrary, I put her directly into my husband's hands. Then my uncle, whom I love dearly, tries to push my head under the slimy water.[50]

Eve White was satisfied with the interpretation that the stagnant water represented her husband's Catholic religious affiliation. A Protestant, she had unwisely promised to raise her children as Catholics, and the uncle in the dream was in reality urging her to keep that promise, which, by then, she bitterly regretted. This interpretation is perfectly correct, but inadequate, since it adds nothing not already present in the conscious attitude at the time. As a much later dream will bear out, the pool also is the feared swamp, and at the same time, the unconscious in which she is about to drown. With such powerful complexes to beleaguer the ego-personality, small wonder the unconscious is likened to a quagmire. Handing up the child shows what she must do for her

---

[50] Op. cit., The Three Faces . . ., p. 16.

child because of her own impending acute illness, but also shows that something of her reborn Self will remain behind after she— Eve White, that is—goes under. (A child is often a symbol for the Self.) A precarious period did follow, where she was hospitalized, and then lived alone in another town, working.

A third personality appeared, dubbed Jane. She was characterized by higher intelligence and generally greater depth of personality than either of the other two, and by a formidable command of language. She began with no knowledge of the others, but gained knowledge of them as time went by. Eve White divorced her husband shortly thereafter.

Remarkable developments then came one after another, prefigured by the following dream sequence (of Jane's, that is):

> For the last few nights I have dreamed that various parts of my body were turning into snakes. Each night more of me is consumed by reptiles. It's getting hard for me even to try to sleep, because I am afraid. . . . Dreaming can become positively maddening. I awaken at night and feel as if all these horrible, unbelievable things are really happening to me. Often it takes some time to convince myself it is only a dream. . . .

> In a dream I was going fishing and Ralph White [the former husband] was walking behind me. He kept repeating the same words, 'Keep walking. Don't look back.' But for some reason I turned and saw him standing there with a long black snake in his hand. . . . Just as I glanced it bit him on the hand. It seemed as if he were trying to protect me.

> A few nights later I was looking through the window in an old deserted hut. In the center of the room was a snake pit. Lots of men were standing around it. All of them had scaly hands—like snakes. Into the room from a side door came Earl [Lancaster, a man Jane shortly married]. They took him and threw him in the pit. When he emerged his hands and feet were black and they also looked like snakes. . . . Two nights later I dreamed the same dream, except this time the man forced into the pit was my doctor [italics in original].[51]

---

[51] *Ibid.*, pp. 175-176.

Snakes usually symbolize a great, possibly dangerous, incompatibility of conscious and unconscious (and not penises, indicating Oedipal and castration anxiety problems, as the Freudians so tiresomely insist). The snakes prefigure a transformation about to take place; the animus, the anonymous men, subject Lancaster and Thigpen to it, for it is in relation to them that the transformation takes place, a bond between the sexes being an analogue for the union of opposites.

Shortly thereafter, on a visit to the parents' house, Jane had occasion to go underneath the house, to fetch a ball Bonnie had thrown there, and this recalled to mind the two early traumatic experiences mentioned above. The two Eves vanished, never to be heard from again. Jane married Earl Lancaster. Bonnie came to live with them, and Jane was touched at how well Earl related to her. Jane was frigid like her predecessors, and this was the central issue in a deterioration of her relationship with Earl. Finally, she tried to commit suicide with sleeping pills, and Earl came along and saved her by administering an emetic. She then had an ecstatic experience of rebirth, in which she felt she was no longer Jane, but all the previous personalities synthesized into one, dubbed Evelyn.[52]

The Jungian analysis of all this is obvious. Starting from the Ego of Eve White, we encounter the problem of integrating and depotentiating the shadow, Eve Black. Consecutive syntheses of unconscious material with the conscious attitude transform the Ego, producing the transitory Jane, and then Evelyn, an approximation of the Self. Her emergence is an ecstatic experience of rebirth.

It is a pity we do not have more dream material to show the rôle of the animus in the transformation. We would expect him to have been fierce and negative while the dissociation was great,

---

[52] Here I am going by her own account (Lancaster, Evelyn, and Poling, James, *The Final Face*, New York: McGraw-Hill, 1958), which differs from the account of Thigpen and Cleckley, who placed the birth of Evelyn at the same time as the "death" of the two Eves, and made no mention of the suicide attempt. I am not in a position to know whether Thigpen and Cleckley fictionalized their account (to protect the anonymity of their client, or for some other reason), or Evelyn and her writer invented some extra details to liven up their otherwise redundant book.

and to have became more human and capable of being related to, after the synthesis. Where it is easy to overlook him in a neurotic case such as this (which, in a way represents a loss of soul), we would expect his manifestations to be glaringly obvious in a schizophrenic case, where the ego-personality loses out, and the contents of the unconscious stream out in their own obscure order.

This expectation is well met in *I Never Promised You a Rose Garden*, since that is the case of a young girl who is literally sucked into a private world, with its own language, "antiphon," and a pantheon of masculine gods or spirits; Anterrabae ("The Falling God" who has no ground under his feet), Lactamaeon ("The Black God," who seems to preside over "changes"), The Censor (a tyrant who divides the world within from the one without, making it impossible for the girl to belong to either), Idat ("The Dissembler"), and Imorkh (a sort of Juggernaut or Golem). There is also a chorus, called (conveniently for us) "The Collect," and the entire private world, known as Yr, is also often referred to by that term.

The girl, Deborah, had had just the kind of contradictory upbringing that constitutes a "double bind," [53] which is widely believed to be a necessary precondition of schizophrenia. Her mother was dominating but rejecting, and showed a combination of fascination and repulsion regarding Deborah, who was a fair, blond child in a household of dark complectioned Jews who were highly self-conscious about their Jewishness, and subjected Deborah to neighborhoods and summer camps where there was open anti-Semitism. Deborah had been operated on for a urethral tumor at age five, and because of the aura of taboo and revulsion her mother attached to that, it represented to Deborah, "being broken into like a looted room, torn apart, scrubbed clean with scouring powder, and reassembled, dead but now acceptable.[54] She felt it set her apart, that a feminine secret that was allowed

---

[53] Bateson, Gregory, et al., "Toward a Theory of Schizophrenia," *Behavioral Science*, Vol. 1, 1956, pp. 251-264.

[54] *Op. cit., I Never Promised You a Rose Garden*, p. 50.

to remain intact in others, had been spoiled in her.[55] We would say that where taboo and constraint alienate the ego-personality from the unconscious, the "double bind" pushes them together, since the distinction between the tensed opposites outside and the ones inside, is lost.

In Deborah's early life, The Collect and the outside were connected by the "midworld." This is strikingly similar to the Ego, except for the lack of recognition of the opposition of qualities between the outside (matter) and the inside (psyche), that is essential to the normal person's adaptation. She came to call herself "Januce," since she had faces pointing in each direction, like the Roman god, Janus, The Censor formed to separate the two worlds, so that by his warnings, Deborah would always be reminded not to talk of The Collect or speak antiphon in the outside world.[56] The rest of the gods would tell her she belonged to them, and not the outside world. When a major portion of her energies was taken up in the activities of The Censor (whose real function was to retard the synthesis of opposites) and the other gods, Deborah's ego-personality was dangerously undermined. Its fragility is pointed to in the gods' repeated reference to her as "Bird-one."

Lactamaeon ("The Black God") told her of *Three Changes and Their Mirrors and then Death* [italics in original]." [57] Death in Yr language was synonymous with "sleep, insanity, or The Pit." The three changes (only one of which occurred prior to the revelation) were the operation, being shamed at the anti-Semitic summer camp, and a suicide attempt during her hospitalization. Each was reflected in some more minor experience, of symbolic significance to Deborah.

Some time after the suicide attempt in the hospital, and during

---

[55] The experience of the womb as a mandala containing one's personal secret, and the production of a child as a liberation or rebirth of the Self, is a universal feminine concern.

[56] The similarity of The Censor to the Freudian superego will doubtless be noted here. It should be pointed out that this Censor is employed in a somewhat different kind of repression than the superego is said to be, and that the essential ethicality, morality, or integrity of Deborah's personality in no way emanates from him.

[57] *Op. cit., I Never Promised You a Rose Garden*, p. 67.

a time of stress caused by the absence of her psychotherapist, Idat (The Dissembler) came to Deborah disguised as a woman dressed in white, and the following "conversation" took place:

> Suffer, Idat. Why do you flow white?
> Shroud and wedding gown, Idat said. Two gowns that are the
>     same gown.
> Behold! Should you not dying, live; and living, die; surrender
>     fighting;
>         and fighting, surrender? My road will give all opposites
>             at the same time,
>         and the same means for the opposite ends,
> I know you from the veil, outward, Idat, Deborah answered.
> I mean that men set backfires, one to kindle yet quench the
>     other.
> Is it applicable also to stone?
> With my help, Idat said. [italics in original][58]

From this Deborah concluded that she could set a resolution of the tension in her in motion by creating a "backfire." She set about making burns on her arm with a cigarette, which also helped to prove to her that she was made of human stuff, and not wholly belonging to Yr.[59]

Perhaps the focal point of the process was the following dream:

> Her dream began with winter darkness. Out of this darkness came a great hand, fisted. It was a man's hand, powerful and hollowed by shadows in the wells between bones and tendons. The fist opened and in the long plain of the palm lay three small pieces of coal. Slowly the hand closed, causing within the fist a tremendous pressure. The pressure began to generate a white heat and still it increased. There was a sense of weighing, crushing time. She seemed to feel the suffering of the coal with her own body, beyond the point of being borne. At last she cried out to the hand, "Stop it! Will you never end it! Even a stone cannot bear to this limit . . . even

---

[58] *Ibid.*, pp. 186-187.

[59] Such ideas about destructive actions are not at all uncommon. When I was a student, I was asked to diagnose a man who had jumped off a bridge, and not noticing that the tide was out, landed in muck (it was the Cuyahoga River in Cleveland, Ohio, which is so polluted as to make one think of the river Styx). He had thought that by doing so, he would be reunited with the mother, and reborn. His motivations were totally different from those of a depressed person who attempts suicide.

a stone . . . !" After what seemed like too long a time for anything molecular to endure, the torments in the fist relaxed. The fist turned slowly and very slowly opened. Diamonds, three of them. Three clear and brilliant diamonds shot with light, lay in the good palm. A deep voice called to her, "Deborah!" and then gently, "Deborah, this will be you." [60]

Thereafter, the disunited pieces came together, smoothly, and not in any sudden, ecstatic experience of rebirth. It was through the gods themselves that the differentiation between The Collect and the outside was made. When Deborah asked Anterrabae to teach her mathematics, he said he couldn't, because she did not already know mathematics. It became a matter of the integration of the two polar worlds, rather than their collision.

A young woman who was a student of mine had had a similar experience of a psychosis experienced as a personal transformation, or rebirth.[61] She, too, had had a schizophrenogenic, "double-bind" childhood, and an early traumatic experience, for which she was made to feel stigmatized and set apart. The active phase of the psychosis took place shortly after the birth of her second child, in her early twenties. She was in psychotherapy, which she started with a curious obliviousness to her therapist as a person. As the therapy progressed, she became aware of a formless, interloping spirit, whom she named, "the Spook." The Spook was experienced as standing between her "I," and a more important spirit, the mysterious, ineffable, "you," whom she came to identify with the therapist. Some excerpts from her diary illustrate:

> What am I screaming at? Go Away! It seems to be a faceless, formless, merciless presence which drives me against my will along a narrow, unyielding path (dance puppet sing for the nice people). Don't you dare to be human. That's what I want to go away.
> And yet I feel that behind this presence there is a gentle, strong, warmth to which I would readily yield, but for the vicious voice in my head that says, "Gotcha!" and, "Don't you dare! He's going to Get you!" Why can't I see around the voice? I know you're there. I can hear you breathing.

---

[60] Op. cit., I Never Promised You a Rose Garden, pp. 242-243.
[61] Anonymous. "The Therapist Experienced as the Self," Unpublished.

61

I kicked the terror in the face. None of your Goddamned business what I've been doing. Go away and leave me alone. It will be back, and I need reinforcement. But I am stronger, and I have a human hand to hold now.

As the terror consumes itself, I will incorporate you. It will be nothing. We will be everything. It's happening fast and strong now. Sometimes the pressure on my head is almost unbearable as I force the walls to yield. But sometimes I can almost see daylight. And I can almost smell the green of Spring.

"Happy Birthday To Me." . . . I've just noticed that I've stopped writing to the mysterious You. It's *ME!* [italics in original].

Here, as with Deborah and her Censor, an evil spirit has attracted so much of the total personality's libido to itself that the ego-personality is undermined, and the integration of the opposites, stopped. When the evil Spook is confronted (depotentiated by insight), synthesis can resume. Where the healing effect of the therapists in the other two cases was, at most, obscure, here we see that the therapist, who was a man, evoked a soul-projection integral to the process of synthesis. This is the essence of the above mentioned unique reinterpretation of transference. Evoking projections and analyzing them becomes an adjunct of the therapist's technique, if it fits the needs of the particular situation, and only then: *"The transference is like those medicines which are a panacea for one and pure poison for another* [italics in original]." [62]

Just as an ancient Chinese text [63] provided the key to the understanding of the quadrantal circles his patients were producing, another archaic source provided Jung with an interpretation of their transferences and personal syntheses. Accordingly, *The Psychology of the Transference* [64] is probably the least like what the title leads one to expect, of all Jung's books; it is a book about alchemy, including only three brief references to therapy cases.

[62] C. W., vol. 16, Foreword before par. 353. *The Psychology of the Transference.*

[63] Wilhelm, Richard. *The Secret of the Golden Flower: A Chinese Book of Life.* New York: Harcourt, Brace, and World, 1962.

[64] C. W., vol. 16, pars. 353-539.

Most moderns think only of charlatans, deceiving people into thinking gold can be made from base metal, when they hear of alchemy. Actually, relatively little of the alchemists' efforts were carried out in the laboratory, since their success in dealing with actual chemical reactions was so necessarily limited; that is probably also the reason for their having shrouded their work assiduously in obscurity and secrecy. Instead, alchemy became a matter of philosophical speculation about the combination of opposites, the chemical reactions they knew about (such as acid-base; salt-water reactions, or the production of liquid mercury from its brown, powdery oxide) providing a receptacle for their projections. The heating of chemicals corresponded to the tension a person feels when a transformation takes place, and the ultimate product of the transformation was variously seen as gold, mercury, an incorruptible philosophers' stone, or an *elixir vitae*, since these were thought to be arcane substances with both spiritual and material qualities.

*The Psychology of the Transference* is mostly devoted to the interpretation of an old alchemical text, *Rosarium Philosophorum*, which is a book of sexual analogues of the conjunction of opposites. The mating of a king and queen, or Sol and Luna, occurring in many different stages along the way to a purer arcane substance, is depicted in ten pictures. They merge into a two-headed bisexual being, die, and experience a heavenly rebirth in that form. The paradoxicalness of this hermaphrodite points to the impossibility of the marriage with one's anima perfect completeness would represent. Such a union would be a self-fertilization, and therefore illegitimate. This is shown by the widespread existence of incest taboos (and of masturbation taboos, for that matter). Jung discusses this in his commentary to the second of the ten pictures, which depicts a king and queen facing one-another, each holding the other's left hand, with a dove flying over them:

> As regards the psychology of this picture, we must stress above all else that it depicts a human encounter where love plays the decisive part. The conventional dress of the pair suggests an equally conventional attitude in both of them. Convention still separates them and hides their natural real-

ity, but the crucial contact of left hands points to something "sinister," illegitimate, morganatic, emotional, and instinctive, i.e., the fatal touch of incest and its "perverse" fascination. At the same time the intervention of the Holy Ghost [the dove] reveals the hidden meaning of the incest, whether of brother and sister or of mother and son, as a repulsive symbol for the *unio mystica*. Although the union of close blood relatives is everywhere taboo, it is yet the prerogative of kings (witness the incestuous marriages of the Pharaohs, etc.). Incest symbolizes union with one's own being, it means individuation or becoming a self, and because this is so vitally important, it exerts an unholy fascination—not, perhaps, as a crude reality, but certainly as a psychic process controlled by the unconscious, a fact well known to anybody who is familiar with psychopathology. It is for this reason, and not because of occasional cases of human incest, that the first gods were believed to propagate their kind incestuously.[65]

From this, we see that Freud was not so wrong to emphasize sexuality in general, and the urge to incest (the Oedipus complex) in particular. The accusation that Jung set out to create a psychology pleasing to those who found the sexual theory distasteful does not hold; his turns out to be just as sexy a viewpoint in the last analysis. We also see how alchemy stays on that topic, even when it wanders away from chemistry altogether. The concerns of the alchemists are epitomized, if not typified, in the following extract from the treatise *Ars Chemica*, which, in the light of the foregoing, should need no interpretation, except that it has to do with the events of Eastertide:

> Our precious stone, that was cast upon the dung-heap, is altogether vile. . . . But when we marry the crowned king with the red daughter, she will conceive a son in the gentle fire, and shall nourish him through our fire. . . . Then is he transformed, and his tincture remains red as flesh. Our son of royal birth takes his tincture from the fire, and death, darkness, and the waters flee away. The dragon shuns the light of the sun, and our dead son shall live. The king shall come forth from the fire and rejoice in the marriage. The hidden things shall be disclosed, and the virgin's milk be whitened. The son is become a warrior fire and surpasses the

---

[65] *Ibid.*, par. 419.

tincture, for he himself is the treasure and himself is attired in the philosophic matter. Come hither, ye sons of wisdom, and rejoice, for the dominion of death is over, and the son reigns; he wears the red garment, and the purple is put on.[66]

\*     \*     \*

Individuation, being concerned with personal transformation and rebirth, pertains directly to religion. The problem of spritual development that, for Jung, characterized the second half of a properly lived life, is a religious problem, and not only in Christianity, where the emphasis on rebirth is so paramount.

Standing midway between the one extreme of accepting a particular religious creed, and the other, of reducing religion to a mere projection of human wishes and fears, Jung's attitude toward religion has provoked considerable misunderstanding. When he was interviewed by John Freeman of the BBC in 1959, Jung replied to the question whether he believed in God or not, "I do not believe, I know," and said, by way of clarification later in the interview: "I don't believe. I must have a reason for a certain hypothesis. Either I know a thing [or I don't], and when I know it, I don't need to believe it." This was actually a recitation of the Gnostic Creed,[67] which gets at the truth paradoxically, by being a creed that nullifies all creeds. But the British television viewers did not know that, and there was a flood of perplexed letters from those who thought they had heard religion reduced to psychology.

Having said that ". . . an archetype [i.e., an imprint] presupposes an imprinter," [68] and thought that the known would somehow be incomplete without a knower, Jung could hardly be a disbeliever in God. As Jung knew Him to be, however, God was not the object of the kind of faith that can be undermined by a

---

[66] Quoted in C. W., vol. 12, par. 454. *Psychology and Alchemy*, 2nd. ed.

[67] The Gnostics were an early Christian sect whose religious knowledge came from experience, or revelation, rather than from authority or belief, prefiguring Jung's empirical, scientific attitude toward the question. Jung wore a Gnostic signet ring on his left hand, which is visible in many pictures of him, and for a time was in possession of an important relic parchment, *Evangelium Veritas* (*The Gospel of Truth*), also known as the Jung Codex (Zürich: Rascher Verlag, 1961).

[68] C. W., vol. 12, par. 15. *Psychology and Alchemy* 2nd, ed.

heliocentric theory of the universe, or an evolutionistic view of man's descent from lower primates. Rather, his was a view in which the scientific attitude and the religious one did not contradict: to explain that, it is convenient to make use of Tillich's distinction between ultimate and idolatrous concerns.[69]

*Ultimate* concern is concern with the ineffable meaning beyond man's finite existence. It is concern with the truth that transcends the paradoxes of the human condition, and that is synonymous with God. Symbols were of paramount importance for Tillich, since they point to the ultimate, which defies literal explication. True faith, for Tillich, was the state of being ultimately concerned, so faith was detached from belief for him, as for Jung. *Idolatrous* concern is the misconstruction of some less important concern as ultimate. The misplaced faith that some have invested in the belief that everything could be understood in terms of the natural sciences is an example, as is the invocation of God as legitimizing this or that human enterprise. To be sure, the naïve faith of the literal believer is an idolatrous concern, in this view.

Since the ultimate truth is beyond man's finite, one-sided perspective, parts of the truth will be found in different viewpoints: they are like the blind men who each give a different account of what an elephant is, because one touches the trunk, another the tusks, another, the tail, and so on. Religious creeds provide a structure that some facet of the ultimate human nature can respond to. They provide guides to inner experience, so that the person can integrate it without being inundated by it, or isolated from others by a reality he cannot share. Various Yoga practices, and Catholic dogma are examples of this, and their rigidity has its virtue because of the overwhelming possibilities of the unconscious. Even the sexual theory of Freud has served such a purpose, since it is "an excellent defense against an onslaught of immediate experience [of the unconscious] with its terrible ambiguity." [70]

The paradox of the split between the goodness and evilness in us is probably the most fundamental such ambiguity. Jung's preoccupation with that problem motivated him to write *Answer*

---

[69] Tillich, Paul. *The Dynamics of Faith*. New York: Harper & Row, 1957.
[70] C. W., vol. 11, par. 79. *Psychology and Religion.*

to *Job*,[71] where it is seen as underlying the emergence of Christianity from Judaism. In Judaism, we see the paradox of a God who, if he were both omnipotent and good, would not allow the evil evident to all, to exist. The emphasis is on faith in spite of this, and adherence to ritual, so that one can be good enough for the messiah when he comes. In Christianity a transformation takes place, because the evil that has been dissociated in that way becomes too great a problem for the individual to contend with. The central symbol of Christianity, Christ crucified between two thieves, concretizes the experience of being suspended or torn between the opposites of good and evil, spirituality and worldliness, and ultimacy and immediacy. The symmetrical cross exhibits the symbolism of the numbers three and four, that we have already encountered.[72] His resurrection is a transformation that integrates the evil in men, since they are cleansed of it if they participate in the experience. As they are transformed, they come closer to a condition of Godliness, which, if finite mortals could reach it, would be transcendence of the tension of opposites that characterizes our human condition.[73] The general issue of ultimacy, and the individual one of individuation, merge. Jung expressed the unfolding of this religious and personal development, laced with a little prophecy of his own, which may be being fulfilled in the current resurgence of interest in religion on the part of young people:

> The death or loss must always repeat itself: Christ always dies, and always he is born; for the psychic life of the archetype is timeless in comparison with our individual time-boundness.

---

[71] C. W., vol. 11, pars. 553-758.

[72] Accordingly, the Trinity is another such symbol, that Jung examined at length (C. W., vol. 11, pars. 169-295. A *Psychological Approach to the Trinity*). The irrationality, and yet the pervasiveness of that idea is typical of religious ideas, and could not be so if there were not some human universal to which they point. The frequency with which things occur in threes in Christianity indicates something missing; it most probably refers to the one-sided emphasis on the masculine, which works itself out in the quasi-secular myths of the Virgin that one encounters in Latin countries, strongly contaminated with the attributes of pagan goddesses.

[73] The Buddhist *nirvana* would also be such a state. Jung felt that state had no meaning in human terms, since without tension there would be no consciousness, and without consciousness, no experience of transformation.

According to what laws now one and now another aspect of the archetype enters into active manifestation, I do not know. I only know—and here I am expressing what countless other people know—that the present [1937] is a time of God's death and disappearance. The myth says he was not found where his body was laid. "Body" means the outward, visible form, the erstwhile but ephemeral setting for the highest value. The myth further says that the value rose again in a miraculous manner, transformed. It looks like a miracle, for when a value disappears, it always seems to be lost irretrievably. So it is quite unexpected that it should come back. The three days' descent into hell during death describes the sinking of the vanished value into the unconscious, where, by conquering the power of darkness, it establishes a new order, and then rises up to heaven again, that is, attains supreme clarity of consciousness. The fact that only a few people see the Risen One means that no small difficulties stand in the way of finding and recognizing the transformed value.[74]

Religion, then, is the cultivation of a personal relationship with a dynamic agency beyond one's own individual personality, that is the source of the universals. While, for psychological purposes, we think of it as within us and unconscious, it is experienced as coming into us from without, and surrounding us (and who is to say it does not?). Jung (after R. Otto) referred to that dynamic agency as the *numinosum*, and an experience of someone or something as imbued with its presence, is said to be experience of him or it as *numinous*.[75] Something numinous is experienced as holy, magical, wonderful, terrible, and indescribable, since those are qualities of the ultimate.

Since there are any number of archetypal contents that are not ultimate, but nevertheless lend a quality of fascination when projected, it is perilously easy for religious strivings to be misplaced.[76] It can be very difficult to tell the ultimate concern from the idolatrous one, or the authentic religious striving from its perversion. When a person or an idea is able to exert influence because some

---

[74] C. W., vol. 11, par. 149. *Psychology and Religion.*

[75] *Ibid.*, par. 6.

[76] It is a common error among Jungian enthusiasts, for instance, to refer to any fascination caused by an archetypal projection as numinous, and thus give an aura of nobility to a pathological condition.

archetypal projection is evoked, we often speak of charisma. The particular projection that subjugates one to the literally unholy attraction of another, Jung ascribed to the archetype of the *mana-personality*. The target of the projection of this archetype is seen as ". . . the mighty man in the form of the hero, chief, magician, medicine man, saint, the ruler of men and spirits, the friend of God."[77] The feminine counterpart is the ". . . sublime, matriarchal figure, the Great Mother, the All-Merciful, who understands everything, forgives everything, who always acts for the best, living only for others and never seeking her own interests, the discoverer of the great love. . . ."[78] The person who is susceptible to such a projection, is so because its contents have previously been dissociated; his conscious attitude has tried to tune them out. Dissociation leads to invasion. The person who evokes the projection does so because his Ego is so strongly identified with the archetype of the mana-personality that he is possessed by it, and his individual personality is displaced into the background; such a person would be diagnosed as paranoid. A group of people who share dissociations in common, and a charismatic leader who can trigger an invasion by the dissociated contents, are the basic ingredients of mass hysteria, which we shall cover in chapter 5.

All the foregoing points to a universal truth beyond the finite pale of the human condition. It is conceivable that this truth is but a function of the nature of the psyche, that it is "merely psychological," so to speak. Those who are inclined toward that opinion may be a little annoyed with me for linking ultimate concern and the scientific attitude, or attribute it to my being a little carried away with my subject. It is also conceivable that the psyche and the universe are related in ways not obvious to the finite, human viewpoint. There are reasons for thinking so, that come from modern physics. The effects of Jung's attempts to look at psychology from the standpoint of modern physics are the topic of the next chapter.

---

[77] C. W., vol. 7, par. 377. *The Relations Between the Ego and the Unconscious: Two.*

[78] *Ibid.*, par. 379.

CHAPTER 4

# Jung and the Scientific Attitude

"For the unconscious psyche space and time seem to
be relative; that is to say, knowledge finds itself in a
space-time continuum in which space is no longer
space, nor time time." (C. W., vol. 8, par. 912. Synchronicity: an Acausal Connecting Principle)

When we ask ourselves whether there can be valid occult phenomena, it is really a solution to the old mind-body conundrum that
we seek. The enterprise of science has not shed much light on the
question, how mind and the physical body interact; maybe it is a
little consoling, then, that when we turn from that question to the
one of psyche interacting with aspects of reality other than the
body, we do not get much further into the dark.

Since Jung went very far afield of the assumptions for which the
familiar, materialistic aspect of science calls, it is important for us
to appreciate the extreme, skeptical, toughminded standpoint he
started from, vis-à-vis occult phenomena. We have already noted
how very early he ascribed spiritualistic phenomena to the activity
of autonomous complexes,[1] just as he tried to explain away the
spontaneous production of symbols as cryptmnesia, before ad-
mitting to the necessity of an hypothesis like that of the collective
unconscious.[2]

The intimacy of the mind-body relationship is shown in the
highly sensitive indicators of physical pathology Jung found in
psychological phenomena. Every doctor who deals with advanced
cases of alcoholism will agree that a reliable symptom of the syn-

[1] See ch. 1.
[2] See ch. 3, footnote 8.

drome, *delirium tremens*, is hallucinations of little, scurrying animals, usually insects or rodents. These hallucinations are simply part of the universal structure of *delirium tremens*, and are, thus, an archetype. They are the only example I know, where one can define conditions that predictably cause an archetype to manifest itself.

Jung made many diagnoses of oncoming physical illness on the basis of such symbols. The little animals of *delirium tremens*, the invertebrates in particular, point to problems with the more primitive parts of the nervous system: ". . . the serpent very often represents the cerebro-spinal system, especially the lower centers of the brain, and particularly the medulla oblongata and the spinal cord. The crab, on the other hand, having a sympathetic nervous system only, represents chiefly the sympathicus and para-sympathicus of the abdomen. . . ." [3] From a sequence including a dream of a crab, Jung correctly predicted the collapse of a man who was in a constant state of sympathetic arousal because of unrealistic aspirations he would not adjust.[4] In another case, a seventeen year old girl's dreams of her mother hanged from a chandelier, and then a horse in an apartment living room, that plunged from a balcony to a gory death on the street below, were the first signs of a fatal organic illness that soon developed.[5] (It is easy to imagine what a fiasco the strictly psychological interpretation of such a dream sequence would be; this is the principal reason why psychoanalysis should never be too far removed from medical supervision.) In still another case, one of the very few where prior experience of the dreamer with the archaic symbols produced could definitely be ruled out, a ten year old girl wrote out an amazing compendium of archaic themes of destruction and restoration. "Little or nothing in the symbolism of her dreams points to the beginning of a normal adult life. . . . When I first read her dreams, indeed, I had the uncanny feeling that they suggested impending disaster."[6] She died a year later of an infectious disease.

---

[3] *Op cit., Analytical Psychology* . . ., p. 102.

[4] *Ibid.*, pp. 87-105. Also, C. W., vol. 16, pars. 297-302. "The Practical Use of Dream-Analysis."

[5] C. W., vol. 16, pars. 343-350. "The Practical Use of Dream-Analysis."

[6] *Op. cit., Man and His Symbols*, pp. 69-74.

These cases in themselves place no strain at all on a causal, materialistic view that makes psyche an epiphenomenon of body. They can be accounted for by unconscious, intuitive perceptions of somatic sensations too weak to be found by another means, and serve to warn us not to let our fancy run away with us when we encounter physical sensitivity much greater than we expect. Even the predictive aspect may be thus explained: the little girl did shortly die of an infectious disease, but her dreams may be thought to have been responding to a dubious somatic situation, certain to succumb to the first hazard that came along. The transition from such cases to ones that confound our ability to find casual explanations is almost imperceptible.

A causal explanation becomes more difficult in the following experience Jung had:

> At the beginning of 1944 I broke my foot, and this misadventure was followed by a heart attack. In a state of unconsciousness I experienced deliriums and visions which must have begun when I hung on the edge of death and was being given oxygen and camphor injections. The images were so tremendous that I myself concluded that I was close to death. My nurse afterward told me, "It was as if you were surrounded by a bright glow." That was a phenomenon she had sometimes observed in the dying, she added. . . .

> It seemed to me that I was high up in space. Far below I saw the globe of the earth, bathed in a gloriously blue light. I saw the deep sea and the continents. Far below my feet lay Ceylon, and in the distance ahead of me the subcontinent of India. . . .

> After contemplating it for a while, I turned around. I had been standing with my back to the Indian Ocean, as it were, and my face to the north. Then it seemed to me that I made a turn to the south. Something new entered my field of vision. A short distance away I saw in space a tremendous dark block of stone, like a meteorite. It was about the size of my house, or even bigger. It was floating in space. . . .

> As I approached the steps leading up to the entrance into the rock, a strange thing happened: I had the feeling that everything was being sloughed away; everything I aimed at or wished for or thought, the whole phantasmagoria of earthly existence, fell away or was stripped from me—an extremely painful process. Nevertheless something remained; it was as

if I now carried along with me everything I had ever experienced or done, everything that had happened around me. I might also say: it was with me, and I was it. I consisted of all that, so to speak. I consisted of my own history, and I felt with great certainty: this is what I am. "I am this bundle of what has been, and what has been accomplished.". . .

From below, from the direction of Europe, an image floated up. It was my doctor, Dr. H.—or, rather, his likeness—framed by a golden chain or a golden laurel wreath. I knew at once: "Aha, this is my doctor, of course, the one who has been treating me. But now he is coming in his primal form, as a *basileus* of Kos. [Here Mrs. Jaffé adds the footnote: *"Basileus* —king. Kos was famous in antiquity as the site of the temple of Asklepios, and was the birthplace of Hippocrates."] In life he was an avatar of this *basileus*, the temporal embodiment of the primal form, which has existed from the beginning. Now he is appearing in that primal form." Presumably I too was in my primal form, though this was something I did not observe but simply took for granted. As he stood before me, a mute exchange of thought took place between us. Dr. H. had been delegated by the earth to deliver a message to me, to tell me that there was a protest against my going away. I had no right to leave the earth and must return. The moment I heard that, the vision ceased.

I was profoundly disappointed, for now it all seemed to have been for nothing. The painful process of defoliation had been in vain, and I was not to be allowed to enter the temple, to join the people in whose company I belonged. . . .

I felt a violent resistance to my doctor because he had brought me back to life. At the same time, I was worried about him. "His life is in danger, for heaven's sake! He has appeared to me in his primal form! When anybody attains this form it means he is going to die, for already he belongs to the 'greater company'!" Suddenly the terrifying thought came to me that Dr. H. would have to die in my stead. I tried my best to talk to him about it, but he did not understand me. Then I became angry with him. "Why does he always pretend he doesn't know he is a *basileus* of Kos? And that he has already assumed his primal form? He wants to make me believe that he doesn't know!" That irritated me. My wife reproved me for being so unfriendly to him. She was right; but at the time I was angry with him for stubbornly refusing to speak of all that had passed between us in my vision. "Damn it all, he

73

ought to watch his step. He has no right to be so reckless! I want to tell him to take care of himself." I was firmly convinced that his life was in jeopardy.

In actual fact I was his last patient. On April 4, 1944—I still remember the exact date—I was allowed to sit up on the edge of my bed for the first time since the beginning of my illness, and on this same day Dr. H. took to his bed and did not leave it again. I heard that he was having intermittent attacks of fever. Soon afterward he died of septicemia. He was a good doctor; there was something of the genius about him. Otherwise he would not have appeared to me as a prince of Kos.[7]

Jung had many other experiences that seemed to go beyond sense-based intuition. For instance, in 1913 he had a persistent series of dreams of floods and cold waves covering Europe.[8] At that time, people had vague conscious fears of revolution, but hardly any of an impending war. Jung thought they pointed to an oncoming psychosis in himself, until the war actually broke out, and some similar predictive dreams of another person came to light.

He had some spiritualistic experiences, of which two are particularly impressive: In 1923 he began building his famous tower in Bollingen, and just before the initial excavations were made his eldest daughter came to him and criticized the project, saying that there were corpses about. In the excavation itself, the remains of a French soldier of Napoleonic times was found, which Jung gave a proper burial with a headstone.[9] Three years earlier, in the summer of 1920, while staying with friends in a rented country house in England, he had a direct encounter with a spirit. On four successive weekends, he heard noises and water dripping in the night, the sources of which he could not discover. He also had an hallucination of the characteristic smell of an advanced, terminal cancer patient, and an apparition of a terrified, dog-sized animal coming into his room. He moved to a different room, and there had the following experience:

---

[7] Op. cit., Memories, Dreams, Reflections, pp. 289-293.

[8] Ibid., pp. 175-176.

[9] Ibid., pp. 231-232.

With effort I opened my eyes. I saw there, *next to me on the* *pillow, the head of an old lady, the right eye wide open* *staring at me. The left half of the face was missing up to the* *eye.* This came so suddenly and unexpectedly that I flew from the bed with a single bound, kindled a light, and spent the rest of the night in an easy chair by candlelight. . . . *I* *felt unnaturally exhausted as I never had felt before.* [italics in original][10]

The apparition lasted only momentarily, and, moving to still another room, Jung was not disturbed again. The house, which was torn down shortly thereafter, had a reputation in the neighborhood for being haunted, and no local servant was willing to be there after dark. Jung never found out its specific history.

Jung also had some experiences with psychokinesis. An early one took place in Freud's study in Vienna in 1909:

> . . . I had a curious sensation. It was as if my diaphragm were made of iron, and were becoming red-hot—a glowing vault. And at that moment there was such a loud report in the bookcase, which stood right next to us, that we both started up in alarm, fearing the thing was going to topple over on us. I said to Freud: "There, that is an example of a so-called catalytic exteriorization phenomenon."
>
> "Oh come," he exclaimed. "That is sheer bosh."
>
> "It is not," I replied."You are mistaken, Herr Professor. And to prove my point I now predict that in a moment there will be another such loud report!" Sure enough, no sooner had I said the words than the same detonation went off in the bookcase. To this day I do not know what gave me this certainty. But I knew beyond all doubt that the report would come again.[11]

This was reminiscent of the inexplicable cracking of the top of a table in his mother's house, that had been in the family for seventy years, followed shortly by the shattering of a bread knife

---

[10] Moser, Fanny. *Spuk: Wahrheit order Irrglaube*, vol. 1. Boden bei Zürich: Gyr Verlag, 1950, p. 257. Jung's contribution is scheduled to appear in C. W., vol. 18. (My translation of the passage.)

[11] *Op. cit., Memories, Dreams, Reflections*, pp. 155-156.

in a basket in the summer of 1898.[12] A final example comes from Jung's practice, late in his life:

> My example concerns a young woman patient. . . . I was sitting opposite her one day, with my back to the window, listening to her flow of rhetoric. She had had an impressive dream the night before, in which someone had given her a golden scarab—a costly piece of jewelry. While she was still telling me this dream, I heard something behind me gently tapping on the window. I turned around and saw that it was a fairly large flying insect that was knocking against the window-pane from outside in the obvious effort to get into the dark room. This seemed to me very strange. I opened the window immediately and caught the insect in the air as it flew in. It was a scarabaeid beetle, or common rosechafer (*Cetonia aurata*), whose gold-green color most nearly resembles that of a golden scarab. I handed the beetle to my patient with the words, "Here is your scarab."[13]

Such experiences point to an interrelatedness of psyche, body, and the universe that transcends our normal viewpoint, and allows for the existence of a reality outside time and space, and not governed by cause and effect. The altered characters of time, space, cause, and effect in dreams suggest such a side to reality; it is as if the psyche were partly to be found in such a different reality, and lived partly outside time and space. That part is necessarily unconscious, since *it lacks the properties of consciousness that time and space represent*; that part may very well have interface with hidden things and with other psyches, of a kind that contradicts our conscious expectations.

In the nineteenth century, when it seemed that the Newtonian view of matter in Euclidean space, governed by energy that was always conserved in some manner was all there was to reality, one had no choice but to dismiss strange experiences such as Jung and countless others have had, as illusion or error. The advent of modern physics, showing time to be a function of velocity so that there are no such things as simultaneity and instantaneous space, showing matter and energy to be a function of each other, and casting doubt (through the Heisenberg irregularity principle) on

---

[12] *Ibid.*, pp. 105-106.
[13] C. W., vol. 8, par. 982. "On Synchronicity."

the doctrine of determinism, has massively undercut the certain knowledge we thought we had of what "reality" is. While it would be beyond the scope of this work (and my competence) to detail the alterations of our world-view entailed by modern physics, I believe it can suffice for our present purposes to say modern physics has undergone a process of divergence, opening up a host of mind-boggling possibilities that so far do not lend themselves to a compact, unified view, and that *do not rule out the possibility of a relatedness in the universe, that is outside time and space, and irrelevant to cause and effect.*[14]

Discounting the cranks who inevitably take up such ideas, willingness to consider the validity of parapsychological phenomena seems to be the greatest in those attuned to modern physics.[15] Jung's early exposure to it, arising from his acquaintance with Einstein in the early twenties,[16] had a crucial formative effect on his thinking. Already before 1930, he had coined the term *synchronicity*, by which he meant a meaningful coincidence of events not related by cause and effect. Thirty years later, after much more experience, the advent of J. B. Rhine's parapsychology

---

[14] Excellent treatments of modern physics for the non-mathematical are *The Universe and Dr. Einstein* by Lincoln Barrett (New York: Mentor, 1957) and *The Philosophical Impact of Contemporary Physics* by Milic Capek (Princeton, N. J.: D. Van Nostrand, 1961).

[15] Arthur Koestler, in *The Roots of Coincidence* (New York: Random House, 1972), lists a veritable *Who's Who* of famous physicists who have been officers of the British Society for Psychical Research (pp. 31-34), to show the affinity of the two topics.

[16] In a letter dated February 25, 1953, to Dr. Carl Selig, Jung wrote: "Professor Einstein was my guest on several occasions at dinner, when, as you have heard, Adolf Keller was present on one of them and on others Professor Eugen Bleuler. . . . These were very early days when Einstein was developing his first theory of relativity. He tried to instill into us the elements of it, more or less successfully. As non-mathematicians, we psychiatrists had difficulty in following his argument. Even so, I understood enough to form a powerful impression of him. It was above all the simplicity and directness of his genius as a thinker that impressed me mightily and exerted a lasting influence on my own intellectual work. *It was Einstein who first started me off thinking about a possible relativity of time as well as space, and their psychic conditionality.* More than thirty years later this stimulus led to my relation with Professor W. Pauli and to my thesis of psychic synchronicity. With Einstein's departure from Zürich my relation with him ceased, and I hardly think he has any recollection of me. [my italics] (*Op. cit., C. G. Jung: Letters.*)

experiments at Duke University, and his collaboration with the physicist Wolfgang Pauli,[17] he ventured a more precise definition: "Synchronicity . . . *means the simultaneous occurrence of a certain psychic state with one or more external events which appear as meaningful parallels to the momentary subjective state—and, in certain cases, vice versa.* [my italics]" [18]

The statement made by this principle is essentially negative. A timeless, spaceless reality beyond our subjective experience is intimated. We are tempted to call it eternal and infinite, though those attributions are more irrelevant than wrong. The mathematical inferences of the physicist and the direct experience of psychic phenomena are clues to it, but anything more than a fleeting knowledge of it eludes us.[19] No positive explanation of the source of parapsychological phenomena is offered; the principle shows us what they are not, but not what they are.

Since the hidden reality is neither physical nor psychic, the mind-body dilemma becomes irrelevant where parapsychological phenomena are concerned. The psychophysiological model, fruitful within its limitations just as Newtonian-Euclidean physics is within its, becomes inadequate, and we lack a more comprehensive one with which to replace it. Accordingly, where it sufficed to think of the archetype as some sort of physiological structure for the purposes of the preceeding chapters, we must here abandon that idea. We are confronted with a reality that (barring some stupendous, unforseen breakthrough) is unknowable and irrepresentable, which Jung called *psychoid*.[20] The ultimate source of order and of experience is psychoid, and appropriately Jung's pupil, Aniela Jaffé, has referred to the psychoid archetype, and called it the "archetype per se."[21]

We have come quite a distance from naïve experience to the

---

[17] Jung, C. G. and Pauli, W. *The Interpretation of Nature and the Psyche.* New York: Bollingen Foundation, 1955. Jung's contribution to this also appears as C. W., vol. 8, pars. 816-968. *Synchronicity.* . . .

[18] C. W., vol. 8, par. 850. *Synchronicity.* . . .

[19] Thus, Kant's view of space and time as subjective categories, with unknowable *noumena* beyond them gains a credence from twentieth century physics, far beyond what was possible in its time.

[20] *Ibid.,* par. 840.

[21] From the *Life and Work of C. G. Jung.* New York: Harper Colophon, 1971, p. 8.

realm of the psychoid, by way of the complexes, the psychological types, and the archetypes of the collective unconscious. Reflecting back, we see that we have been dealing with the data of human experience all along; with the quest to find order in it and render it more understandable. This is the essence of the empirical scientific attitude. Science must be open to its own findings, and absolutely must not ignore them in order to seek a preconceived goal. When the findings undercut all our natural assumptions, and lead us to infer a reality that is inherently incomprehensible, this necessary openness becomes very hard to maintain. If doubt is cast on time, space, and causality, nothing is left but our experience as we find it. Experience, and not quantification, logic, or even explanation, is the common denominator of science. There is no science without a scientist.

The distinguishing feature of Jung's work, then, that recommends it over the other psychologies I am familiar with, is that *it finds out the interesting things in it, rather than proceeding from them as assumptions.* Avoidance of misplaced faith in preconceived assumptions is its hallmark, and the chief reason for denying that Jung's interest in religion was attributable to mysticism, his fascination with alchemy, to obscurantism, and his interest in Plato and Kant, to his being a philosopher rather than a scientist. In one of his few comments on this, he said: ". . . I am not [a philosopher]. I do not 'posit' the unconscious. . . . If I posited the archetypes, for instance, I would not be a scientist but a Platonist."[22] Much later he said, "From a philosophical standpoint my empirical concepts would be logical monsters, and as a philosopher I should cut a very sorry figure."[23]

Such a standpoint obviously calls for extreme caution in departing from the causal assumptions that *do* account for the vast majority of our experience. That Jung was cautious about it is shown in the extreme slowness with which he moved away from his early totally skeptical view of occult phenomena.[24] It is also shown in a sort of Occam's Razor (or Lloyd Morgan's Canon) of

[22] Letter to Arnold Künzli, February 4, 1943 *Op. cit., C. G. Jung: Letters.*
[23] C. W., vol. 11, par. 460. Foreword to White's "God and the Unconscious."
[24] See chapter 1.

79

synchronicity he expressed, where synchronicity should be called upon as an explanation only where a causal one cannot account for what is observed: ". . . wherever a cause is even remotely thinkable, synchronicity becomes an exceedingly doubtful proposition."[25]

The scientific attitude also calls for research supplementing the generalization from experience that was Jung's main method, and we find three separate efforts in his late work to research the question of synchronicity: some informal trials with *I Ching* divinations, a quantitative test of some astrological predictions (complete with tests of statistical significance), and a survey-content-analysis study of spirit phenomena, which was actually carried out by his pupil, Aniela Jaffé because Jung's attention was diverted to other things.[26]

*I Ching*, the Chinese Book of Changes, is an oracle consulted by a lottery choice from among sixty-four possible interpretations. There are persistent reports of amazing correspondence between the answers and questions put to *I Ching*, that chance could scarcely account for. The immediate inclination of the western mind is to compare this with psychokinesis (PK), the physical, willful influence of mind over matter. Rhine and others have made some suggestive efforts to reproduce the phenomena in the laboratory, with subjects trying to influence dice throws and the like through concentration. Causally conceived laboratory experiments have limited applicability to *I Ching* in our context, since the view of a temporal existence characterized by the tension of polar opposites, contrasted by an ultimate reality beyond the pale of time, space, and causality, with which we have been tinkering, dovetails with the Taoist system of thought underlying *I Ching*.

The keystone of the Taoist system is the conjunction of the opposites, *Yin*, the receptive, dark, feminine principle, and *Yang*, the creative, bright, masculine principle. Proceeding from that

---

[25] C., W., vol. 8, par. 876. *Synchronicity.* . . .

[26] Jung also did a survey study of U.F.O. reports (C. W., vol. 10, pars. 589-824. *Flying Saucers: A Modern Myth of Things Seen in the Skies.*), that does not pertain much to synchronicity. It is covered in the next chapter.

basic dichotomy, the symbolic trigrams are made, that form the basis of *I Ching*. Since three dichotomies yield eight ($2^3$) possibilities, there are eight trigrams. These are typically symbolized as a family consisting of a father, a mother, three sons, Arousing, Abysmal, and Still respectively, and three daughters, Gentle, Clinging, and Joyous, respectively. The conjunctions of these yield the sixty-four hexagrams ($8^2$ or $2^6$ possibilities).[27] The hexagrams are signs of situations, symbolized by a variety of images, frequently including weather conditions, seasons of the year, alchemical descriptions, and interpersonal situations. A great deal of subjective interpretation is needed to apply them to the questions asked, and of course a great deal of the effect is due to the mere evocation of projections that bring new understanding.

The understanding is not analytic, but rather a glimpse of the totality of the situation, a symbolic cross-section as it were. An intricate procedure involving the casting of yarrow stalks was originally used to select the particular hexagram to answer a particular question; however, this has largely been supplanted by a less cumbersome procedure, where three coin throws are needed to determine a trigram, and six for a hexagram. The throws of coins or stalks are thought to derive their order by being caught up in the totality of the situation in which they take place. Accordingly, Taoism is a naturalistic view, advocating harmony with the nature within and without that comprises the Tao, or the Way. The distinction it occurs to the western mind to make between the mere projection and the genuine synchronistic experience loses its meaning, since the sequential, causal aspect of the total situation recedes into the background.

For a long time before the advent of the Wilhelm translation Jung was familiar with *I Ching* through the English translation by James Legge, and as early as 1920, he would sit under an old pear tree at his house in Bollingen, and consult it. While he mentions in passing a number of striking "hits," the only detailed description he gives is of two trials where he asked *I Ching*

---

[27] See Wilhelm, Richard, Trans. *I Ching* or *Book of Changes*. Retranslated by Cary F. Baynes. New York: Bollingen Foundation, 1967, pp. xlvii-lxi.

about his intention to write a foreword to the English retranslation of the Wilhelm translation.[28]

The first hexagram Jung obtained (using the coin procedure) was *Ting* (#50), The Cauldron. In the text, the *ting* is a ritual cooking vessel, capable of providing spiritual nourishment, but in derelict condition, sitting with its legs upturned. In answer to the question, *I Ching* had replied that it was a valuable source, needing rehabilitation.

In referring to itself, *I Ching* highlighted the tendency to personify it. It is as if one entered into a dialogue with a person of immense age and wisdom when one consults it. "I questioned *I Ching* as one questions a person whom one is about to introduce to friends: one asks whether or not it will be agreeable to him. In answer, *I Ching* tells me of its religious significance, of the fact that at present [1948] it is unknown and misjudged, of its hope of being restored to a place of honor—this last obviously with a sidelong glance at my as yet unwritten foreword. . . ." [29]

Jung rephrased the question more directly, and the answer was *K'an* (hexagram # 29), The Abysmal (Water), and particularly the verse:

> Forward and backward, abyss on abyss.
> In danger like this, pause at first and wait,
> Otherwise you will fall into a pit in the abyss.
> Do not act in this way.

Formerly I would have accepted unconditionally the advice, "Do not act in this way," and would have refused to give my opinion of the *I Ching*, for the sole reason that I had none.

---

[28] C. W., vol. II, pars. 964-1018. "Foreword to the 'I Ching'." N.B.: Mrs. Baynes' translation of the German manuscript of the foreword Jung provided for her retranslation of Wilhelm's work diverges considerably from the original, and conceals much of Jung's enthusiasm. For instance the sentence, "It was the subjective conviction alone, that there was 'something to' the *I Ching*, that induced me to write this foreword," is deleted altogether from the English. (Jung, C. G., *Zur Psychologie westlicher und östlicher Religion*. Zürich: Rascher Verlag, 1963, par. 1000. My translation of the quote.) I am indebted to Mrs. Aniela Jaffé for pointing this out to me.
[29] *Ibid.*, par. 983.

But now the counsel may serve as an example of the way in which the *I Ching* functions. It is a fact that if one begins to think about it, the problems of the *I Ching* do represent "abyss on abyss," and unavoidably one must "pause at first and wait" in the midst of the dangers of limitless and uncritical speculation; otherwise one really will lose one's way in the darkness. Could there be a more uncomfortable position intellectually than that of floating in the thin air of unproven possibilities, not knowing whether what one sees is truth or illusion?[30]

Thus, the answers encouraged Jung to act to aid in the rehabilitation of *I Ching* but warned him of the attendant difficulties. The second hexagram said in addition:

If you are sincere, you have success in your heart,
And whatever you do succeeds.

It pushed him to make a judgment one is always hard put to make about oneself, particularly at the time. It is typical of *I Ching* to answer by inducing one to ask the right question.[31]

Trials with *I Ching* leave one with little more than the subjective conviction that something relevant has taken place.

---

[30] *Ibid.*, par. 1003.

[31] I repeated Jung's example before writing this section, asking *I Ching* twice, "Will my book accomplish what I wish it to?" The first answer was *Ming I* (hexagram #36), Darkening of the Light.

In adversity

It furthers one to be persevering.
. . . .
The light has sunk into the earth:
The Image of DARKENING OF THE LIGHT
Thus does the superior man live with the great mass:
He veils his light, yet still shines.

The relevance of this to this project, the summarization of the neglected and misunderstood work of another, is obvious. The commentary also said, ". . . a man of dark nature is in a position of authority and brings harm to the wise and able man." This I took as a reference to a situation in the university where I teach, which has diverted much of my energy from this work. The second answer was *Wu Wang* (hexagram # 25), Innocence (The Unexpected).

Jung wanted something that could be quantified, and found it in the horoscopes of married people. The astrological literature indicates that marriages are most likely under certain astrological conditions; particularly the sun-moon conjunction, the moon-moon conjunction, and the moon-ascendent conjunction.[32] Using random pairings of men's horoscopes with those of women other than their wives, a control group of unmarried pairs was created. A list of fifty aspects traditionally said to be characteristic of marriage was constructed, and percentages and frequency indices were computed for each aspect and each group. This was initially done with a batch of 180 married pairs, then with a second batch of 220, and finally with the two batches pooled. The average frequency indices in all groupings were no higher than chance.[33] There were, however, some eye-opening details. A rank ordering of the frequencies for married people corresponded pretty well to an ordering of the chosen aspects from the most strongly indicative of marriage to the least so; the three aspects singled out for particular mention above had the highest frequencies, and were, in themselves, an extremely (astronomically!) improbable result. Not claiming to have proved anything about astrology, Jung put

---

> INNOCENCE. Supreme success.
> Perseverance furthers.
> If someone is not as he should be,
> He has misfortune,
> And it does not further him
> To undertake anything.

The original question had been deliberately phrased to avoid begging the important question, whether my desire to write a worthwhile book was ahead of my desire to derive personal success from the publication of a book, as I wished it to be. The *I Ching* responded by coupling that issue to another which had seemed unrelated, my inability to progress as fast as I wished to, with this book. Both questions turned out to have the same answer. I was to persevere, but not so much as to interfere with the project's maturing of itself.

[32] C. W., vol. 8, par. 869. *Synchronicity.* . . .

[33] This was determined by having a mathematician calculate the odds for each percentage and frequency index; the convenient inferential statistics so familiar in America were not used, and there was probably no person readily available who was skilled in them. Inspecting the material given (*Ibid.*, pars. 827-910), I am led to suspect that non-parametric tests would come up significant, if not an analysis of variance.

this one effort of his later life to do a quantitative experiment into perspective:

> . . . on psychological grounds I have discarded the idea that we are dealing with mere chance numbers. In a total picture of natural events, it is just as important to consider the exceptions to the rule as the averages. This is the fallacy of the statistical picture: it is one-sided, inasmuch as it represents only the average aspect of reality and excludes the total picture. The statistical view of the world is a mere abstraction and therefore incomplete and even fallacious, particularly so when it deals with man's psychology. Inasmuch as chance maxima and minima occur, they are *facts* whose nature I set out to explore. [italics in original][34]

The survey study of spirit phenomena stemmed from a request by the editor of the *Schweizerischer Beobachter*, in 1954, that his readers send in accounts of their personal experiences with spirit occurrences. These were forwarded to Jung, who had apparently intended to work on them himself, but later gave them to Mrs. Jaffé, who organized and analyzed them.[35] She found several recurring forms of apparitions, including luminous ghosts, white ghosts, the woman in white, and the spirit manikin. The principal condition for their occurrence was a tense psychological situation, e.g. a complex. The apparition would convey some piece of information, most often of a death, that the person experiencing it had no other way of knowing at the time, thus giving evidence that the phenomenon was more than a mere delusion with an autonomous complex behind it.

Remembering the context of the principle of synchronicity, there is little utility in an either-or distinction between the manifestation of a complex and that of a "genuine" spirit. Much later, Dr. von Franz put the relationship of complexes and spirits into perspective:

> . . . I once was able to observe, in the analysis of a woman whose brother later "disintegrated" into incurable schizo-

---

[34] *Ibid.*, par. 884.
[35] Jaffé, Aniela. *Apparitions and Precognitions*. Hyde Park: University Books, 1963.

phrenia, how part-souls of the brother seemingly brought about parapsychological spook phenomena in her proximity. When I conveyed this to Jung, he told me he had frequently observed such things, and considered it possible for fragmentary complexes of a living person to engage in "spooking"....

The question, so often discussed, whether certain unconscious complexes of the participants or "real spirits" appear in spiritual sessions, would in this view be obsolete; there would simply be autonomous complexes that belong either to living or dead persons. Accordingly, "belong" also really is not correctly formulated, since "autonomous" means, to be sure, that such complexes are not to any great extent attached, but rather are free-floating.[36]

Dr. von Franz also made a generalization about the conditions under which parapsychological phenomena take place, which can be applied to all of the foregoing:

It appears more and more to be confirmed that parapsychological phenomena occur particularly frequently around people *who are impelled by the unconscious to make a step forward in consciousness,* for example, adolescents who need to make the "leap" into adulthood,[37] or creative personalities who need to realize a new accomplishment directed by the unconscious, and all those in serious conflict which could be overcome only through a widening of consciousness. [italics in original][38]

If creative disequilibrium is a precondition for parapsychological experiences, then it is a small wonder that Jung had so many of them. In a letter to J. B. Rhine (May 20, 1935) he wrote: "... I prefer not to communicate too many of my experiences. They would confront the scientific world with too upsetting problems."[39]

---

[36] *Op. cit., Zahl und Zeit,* p. 248. (My translation of the passage.)

[37] An example of this happened to me when I was thirteen years old. A schoolmate and I heard about Dr. Rhine's experiments, and over a period of several days telepathically transmitted letters and numbers for about twenty trials without error. I was actually able to see the correct letters or numbers when I closed my eyes. Weeks later, we were completely unable to duplicate the effect.

[38] *Ibid.,* pp. 204-205.

[39] *Op. cit., C. G. Jung: Letters.*

When he died, a number of people learned of it through dreams and apparitions, according to Mrs. Jaffé, who also reported:

> A couple of hours after his death there was a violent thunderstorm, and lightning struck a tall poplar in the garden beside the lake, where he was accustomed to sitting. The lightning sizzled along the trunk into the ground, displacing the heavy stones of a low parapet. From the open wound it had burned into the bark I cut out a strip of bast. Then the gardener stopped up the wound with pitch, and the tree is still alive today.[40]

These intriguing but inadequate researches lead us back to the main issue: the intimations of an ultimate reality beyond physical time, space, and causality, on the one hand, and the psychic tension of opposites that is our consciousness, on the other. What can such a reality be like? How far back can knowledge push the limits of our finite mortality? Do we continue, in some manner, to exist there after death, in some complete, primal form like the image of the *basileus* of Kos in Jung's vision? These are matters of pure speculation, and accordingly we end our discussion of the fundamentals of Jung's work with two others' efforts to go beyond him in speculation.

The first got its impetus from the following comment by Jung:

> There is something peculiar, one might even say mysterious, about numbers. They have never been entirely robbed of their numinous aura. If, so a text-book of mathematics tells us, a group of objects is deprived of every single one of its properties or characteristics, there still remains, at the end, its number, which seems to indicate that *number* is something irreducible. . . . The sequence of natural numbers turns out to be unexpectedly more than a mere stringing together of identical units: it contains the whole of mathematics, and everything yet to be discovered in this field. . . . That numbers have an archetypal foundation is not, by the way, a conjecture of mine, as we shall see in due course.[41] Hence it is not such

---

[40] Op. cit., *From the Life and Work of C. G. Jung.*, p. 137.

[41] He refers to "The Influence of Archetypal Ideas on the Scientific Theories of Kepler," by Wolfgang Pauli, the latter's contribution to the work they authored together *(Op. cit.),* in which this passage originally appeared.

an audacious conclusion after all if we define number psychologically as an *archetype of order* which has become conscious. [italics in original][42]

Dr. von Franz, who has a gift for mathematics that her teacher lacked, took up this question, and has clarified the rôle of number as follows:

> ... *numbers seem to be a characteristic of matter, as well as to represent an unconscious basis of our mental ordering process.* For this reason, according to Jung, number is the only element that seems suited *to unite the realms of matter and psyche.* It is "real" in a different sense than the archetypal images, because it occurs as quantity in the environment, too, and thereby provides a bridge between the tangible and the imaginary. So for the present, it becomes a still little researched intermediary between myth (psychical) and reality (physical), invented and discovered, quantitative and qualitative, observable and unobservable alike. [italics in original][43]

Dr. von Franz followed up the possible clues to the nature of ultimate reality that are found in the symbolic qualities of numbers. The number one, for example, symbolizes the complete, unitary ultimate reality we have been discussing. It has been represented as a state of Godliness, or a metaphysical primal or final condition, in many religious and alchemical works.[44] Jung called it the *unus mundus*, or unitary world; it is also the unreachable goal of the process of individuation.[45] Translated into mathematics, the *unus mundus* becomes a comprehensive field, or as Dr. von Franz calls it, a oneness-continuum.

> If one looks at the natural numbers as qualitative aspects or configurations of such a oneness-continuum, then the quality of a natural number is not tied to its "units," but rather to its totality alone, which includes an irrational element with it.[46]

---

[42] C. W., vol. 8, par. 870. *Synchronicity*. . . .
[43] *Op. cit., Zahl und Zeit*, p. 55. (My translation)
[44] von Franz, M. L. "Symbols of the 'Unus Mundus.' " In: Wheelwright, Joseph B. Ed. *The Reality of the Psyche*. New York: G. P. Putnam's Sons, 1968.
[45] C. W., vol. 14, par. 662. *Mysterium Coniunctionis*.
[46] *Op. cit., Zahl und Zeit*, p. 67. (My translation)

All the numbers other than one are then disturbances of this field, just as in a different sense, consciousness is a disturbance of it, an area of tension looking for a resolution.

The One itself is necessarily unconscious, unconscious by definition as it were. With the number two, symmetry, opposition, and rhythm come into being, all disturbances on the oneness-continuum. The dimensions of time and space are not yet manifest, so the Two is prior to the advent of consciousness.

> With the two . . . it is primarily a question of the image of a polarity that wants to manifest itself dynamically as an oscillation or a systole-diastole rhythm. It is only its manifold repetition that leaves a "trail," and with it a time or space vector, the third that is not quite explicit in the two, but merely comes along with it implicitly.[47]

The Three, as we have already seen, stands for the mortal condition, the disturbed, intermediate condition to which time and space belong. It is the resultant of polar opposites, and is generated by the opposition of Two. "In the third, the tension resolves itself, while the lost One returns [italics in original]." [48]

The Four is a completeness model, in which the lost One has returned. "One subsumes totalities, Two divides, recapitulates, and generates symmetries, Three lends centers to the symmetries and initiates linear processes, and Four stabilizes totalities through regression to One, and makes individual ones discriminable by describing boundaries, etc." [49] Beginning with five, numbers are less permeated by primitive symbolic properties, although many, like seven, have them.

That numbers possess these properties is unverifiable, and perhaps even incomprehensible. We gain nothing more than an intimation of what could be the case from such discussion. Looking at the tacit properties of numbers, the most explicit things we know, does push us to the limits.

The other speculative attempt to go beyond Jung speaks far more directly to our condition. It grew out of a Canadian psy-

---

47 Ibid., pp. 94-95.
48 Ibid., p. 100.
49 Ibid., p. 75.

chology professor's perplexity with his colleagues, each so bound up in the particular perspective and assumptions of his discipline that the university seemed like a Tower of Babel. The English professor scorned his colleague in the math department for immersing his mind in sterile tautology; the mathematician, in turn, scorned the biologist for relying on unquantifiable concepts; the biologist, who saw no non-biological implications to behavior, had no use for the psychologist; and the psychologist could never understand why an English professor would go such a long way around to describe a character in a novel, when the rubric "paranoiac" or "psychopath" would have been enough. Furthermore, none was superior to the other, or to the average man, in coping with practical problems of life.

The professor, Dr. Joseph Royce,[50] noticed that different criteria seemed to underlie the discrepancies, and that looking at a problem one way seemed to preclude looking at it another. In explaining the criteria, Royce came up with four basic modes, derived from Jung's four functions, that different disciplines employ in different characteristic combinations. These are:

1. Thinking. Deductive coherence and logical interrelation are the objectives when thinking is employed. Mathematics and some specialties in philosophy stress thinking over all the other possibilities, and so are said to be rationalistic disciplines.

2. Feeling. Royce does not use the term in the Jungian sense, but refers instead to intuition and insight as methods of knowing. Art and music are examples of "feeling" disciplines.

3. Sensing. Knowledge of things by having empirical evidence about them, as in at least some phases of every natural science, arises from this criterion.

4. Believing. Since we cannot apply all the other criteria to all the problems we are interested in ourselves, we must accept the word of others on their authority, and make judgments, which are the trustworthy authorities. This is a necessary short-cut in knowing. We must choose the style of knowing that makes sense to us also, and make that a matter of belief. This corresponds roughly to

[50] The Encapsulated Man. Princeton: D. Van Nostrand, 1964, pp. 12-19.

Jung's feeling function, and provides for the subjective aspect of every kind of knowing.

It is easy to see how these combine to provide the foundations for a particular field of knowledge. The natural sciences utilize a combination of thinking and sensing in their quest for verification. The humanistic disciplines mix feeling, thinking, and believing. This is also true of religion, except that the emphasis on believing is more pronounced; it is simple to diagnose the principal difficulties in contemporary organized religions as the result of too much stress on authority and not enough on intuition.

For Royce as for Jung, there is an ultimate reality beyond the finite, mortal pale, where the four kinds of knowledge converge. They are like the parallel lines that do meet in infinity. To conceive of ultimate reality is impossible; to appreciate that it is there is to overcome the one-sided presumptuousness of a particular viewpoint, that Royce calls *encapsulation*. His is a plea against overspecialization, and for academic generalism. While he does not concern himself with personal growth as Jung does, he advocates intellectual completeness.

All these speculations lead to the same obscure destination. It does not matter whether we call it a primal state, a oneness-continuum, or ultimate reality. The discrepancies in man's knowledge are due to his inherent one-sidedness and limitation of perspective. The way science grows by replacing one formulation with a more comprehensive one, by going from the greater to the lesser fiction, implies this limitation and takes it into account. These speculations have carried us very far from the development of the individual and relevancy to the human condition. When pursued to its ultimate extent, Jung's work leads us to very abstruse regions. Having covered all the main parts, we are ready to look at the relevance of the whole.

# CHAPTER 5

# Jung's Social Relevance

"That man alone possesses the primacy of reason is antiquated twaddle. I have even found that men are far more irrational than animals." (Letter to Pastor Arz, April 10, 1933. Op. cit., *C. G. Jung: Letters.*)

Coming back from the cosmic frontiers, we readjust our focus again to the human level. Our detour through ultimate reality returns us to the question of ultimate relevance, the individual and his personal destiny unfolding. What would be the point of such an intricate mass of technical details as we have covered, if it did not show us something of what man is and how he should live?

When the questions, "what is man?" and "how should he live?" are taken up, it cannot help but have political significance. Political ideologies are by nature extraverted, and so received rather little of Jung's predominantly introverted attention. His personal life was thoroughly—a socialist would say callously—bourgeois. It was made so by his particular style, and not by conviction. He explained it, "The daimon of creativity has ruthlessly had its way with me. The ordinary undertakings I planned usually had the worst of it—though not always and not everywhere. By way of compensation, I think, I am conservative to the bone."[1]

But Jung became famous, and the world did not leave him to his preferences. He was part of a time when socially conscious intellectuals were interested in collective, socialistic ideologies. Today, when the most powerful socialist country stands for the persecution of Jews, the use of psychiatry as a means to repress dissent, and the colonial exploitation of East-central Europe, it

---

[1] Op. cit., *Memories, Dreams, Reflections,* p. 358.

92

takes effort to imagine what naïve belief in socialism was like. As early as 1918, Jung saw that the atomization of the individual and the improvement of the quality of life were as polar opposites.[2] Consistently through the years he was against totalitarianism, and for whatever gave the individual the maximum latitude to follow his inner calling. As we shall see, it was his misfortune to be in so conspicuous a position that the totalitarian ideologists of the day either had to insinuate him into their viewpoints, or else discredit him. The incompatibility of Jung's psychology with political ideology generated persistent malicious allegations against him, a story we shall come to presently.

It is obvious that, in Jung's view, a person who cannot pursue his inner striving for individuation because the state makes him its servant will be sick. Nevertheless, we are constantly witnessing such subordination, and even crowds of people looking for it, to escape the stagnancy and absurdity of their individual lives. It seems that people submerged in groups become gullible, deluded, and capable of every kind of foolishness they would know better than, as individuals. Jung's diagnoses of such social pathology have an immense practical significance that has been all but neglected.

The healthy individual, to recapitulate, has an extensive consciousness, well able to withstand being open to the unconscious, in contrast to the neurotic with his brittle, narrow consciousness, and the psychotic, with his besieged, fragmented one. The common denominator of pathological cases is a diminution of consciousness, an *abaissement de niveau mental*. The unconscious is a danger for them; the unconscious contents that would be enriching if the ego-personality were able to assimilate them, invade the reduced consciousness, produce compelling, fascinating illusions, and give shape to irrational behavior.

The collective pathology works in the same way as an individual one, and participation in a collective has the same effect as any individual etiological factor that diminishes the tension of consciousness.

It is a notorious fact that the morality of society as a whole is in inverse ratio to its size; for the greater the aggregation

[2] See C. W., vol. 7, par. 240. *The Relations Between the Ego and the Unconscious: One.*

of individuals, the more the individual factors are blotted out, and with them morality, which rests entirely on the moral sense of the individual and the freedom necessary for this. Hence, man is, in a certain sense, unconsciously a worse man when he is in society than when he is acting alone; for he is carried by society and to that extent relieved of his individual responsibility.[3,4]

He adapted this thesis from the French sociological classic, *The Crowd*, by Gustave Le Bon, who regarded crowds as "only capable of thinking in images . . . only to be impressed by images. It is only images that terrify or attract them and become motives of action."[5] "Contagion" was the explanation offered for the transmission of these ill defined, yet vividly shared images. The weakness of that explanation has generally made social scientists feel excused from taking the thesis seriously. But with the archetypes of the collective unconscious as the source of the unspoken and implicit consensus, it becomes plausible that "contagion" could take place.

Paraphrasing Jung very liberally, mass hysteria or irrational crowd behavior begins with a genuine threat against which the individual has no realistic defense. A vague anxiety or an unidentified intuition that a threat is imminent may be the extent of awareness of it. Archetypal symbolism, much like the contents of a prophetic dream, is projected onto real people and things, and acted out. The actions will be irrational and immoral. Rationalizations will be found, and a tenuous equilibrium established between the collective delusion and the critical demands of what is left of individual consciousness. Two examples of the process were studied by Jung: the flying saucer scares of the fifties, and the Nazi era in Germany. We will treat the latter topic at length,

---

[3] This has been demonstrated empirically by experimental social psychologists under the rubric, "risky shift phenomenon." Decisions taken by groups where all share in the responsibility are found to be more daring and risky, and less restrained by moral standards, than comparable decisions the same persons take as individuals. (A good review and bibliography may be found in Brown, Roger, *Social Psychology*, New York: The Free Press, 1965, p. 656ff.)

[4] Op. cit., *The Relations Between the Ego and the Unconscious*.

[5] New York: Compass Books, 1960, p. 68.

since it has also been the focus of scurrilous allegations made against him, that one still hears in cocktail party conversations.

## THE FLYING SAUCER SCARES
## AND THE COLD WAR

As we established in chapter 2, one process underlies both the correct and the deluded apprehension of a person's surroundings, namely the projection of archetypes. The greater the discrepancy between the conscious attitude and the unconscious potential for a better understanding, the more unruly the projection. When an aspect of an individual's shadow finds an echo in the shadows of his fellows, an unconscious cooperation in creating a social problem may occur. The trouble is presumed to be due to external forces, and the participants never see that the culprit is in them. If suitable targets for the projection of this inner culprit are found, they become scapegoats, or at least objects of prejudice.

> Projections have what we might call different ranges, according to whether they stem from merely personal conditions or from deeper collective ones. Personal repressions and things of which we are unconscious manifest themselves in our immediate environment, in our circle of relatives and acquaintances. Collective contents, such as religious, philosophical, political and social conflicts, select projection-carriers of a corresponding kind—Freemasons, Jesuits, Jews, Capitalists, Bolsheviks, Imperialists, etc. In the threatening situation of the world today [1958], when people are beginning to see that everything is at stake, the projection-creating fantasy soars beyond the realm of earthly organizations and powers into the heavens, into interstellar space, where the rulers of human fate, the gods, once had their abode in the planets. Our earthly world is split into two halves, and nobody knows where a helpful solution is to come from. . . . Under these circumstances it would not be at all surprising if those sections of the community who ask themselves nothing were visited by "visions," by a widespread myth seriously believed in by some and rejected as absurd by others. Eye-witnesses of unimpeachable honesty announce the "signs in the heavens" which they have seen "with their own eyes," and the marvelous things they have experienced which pass human understanding.[6]

---

[6] C. W., vol. 10, par. 610. *Flying Saucers: A Modern Myth of Things Seen in Skies.*

The principal projection Jung treated was the sightings of un-identified flying objects (UFOs), themselves. Any aware person who lived through the times in question can confirm that the incidence of these, and the degree of publicity they received, were in direct proportion to the intensity of uncertain danger of im-pending war, prior to WWII, and much more intensely during the height of the cold war in the middle fifties.

In his study,[7] Jung devoted most of his attention to the circular shape of the objects, since these are obviously mandalas,[8] implicat-ing the process of individuation itself in the drama. Outer space is, equally obviously, an analogue for the unconscious, the earth representing the ego-complex, and other objects in it, other com-plexes in some sort of relationship to consciousness; the correspond-ence to our didactic model from chs. 1 and 2, above, is literally, even comically exact. Since the alien visitors connected with these complexes come from a primitive layer of the psyche, they often turn out to be insect or reptile-like, lacking warm blood or a cere-brospinal nervous system. This is typically true if they represent the unconscious destructiveness in us, which is the basis of all wars, that we are doomed to live out if we do not depotentiate it by making it conscious. The visitors may, on the other hand, be helpful, even angelic, projections of the Self or of God. Like every other myth, the arrival of visitors from outer space expresses a personal transformation taking place, and loses its meaning if the mistake of taking it literally is made.

Three familiar examples of the flying saucer myth in the con-text of American society are the end-of-the-world cult in Min-nesota studied by Festinger, the widespread panic that resulted from Orson Welles' "War of the Worlds" broadcast on Halloween night, 1938, and the camp classic, "Flash Gordon." While Jung did not explore any of these in detail, they closely parallel the ones in his study; we cover them here in order to get as close as we can to application of the understanding they shed.

Sometime in the middle fifties, a team from the University of Minnesota infiltrated a group prophesying that flying saucers would rescue them from the impending destruction of the earth

[7] Ibid.
[8] See ch. 3.

96

by flood.[9] The source of the prophecies was "extraterrestrial" messages received in automatic writing and voices by a housewife. The investigators restricted their attention to the tendency of the belief, contrary to common sense expectations, to get stronger as portions of its content were disconfirmed. They reported the details of the prophecies, which were incidental insofar as they were concerned, without comment.

The prophetess was very similar to the psychic medium Jung observed in his youth. At first, she received spirit visitations from her deceased father, and an unknown "Elder Brother." She then started taking messages sent by "Sananda," a superior being from another world. It seemed that the earth people's experiments with atomic bombs had cracked a sedimentary shield between his galaxy and earth. He gave her instructions about preparations for visitations, and the eventual removal of a few "chosen" to safety before the wicked earth destroyed itself. Pronouncements about the geophysical prehistory of the universe (not unlike those of Jung's medium) were also received. The prophetess gathered a group of believers, which became more cohesive and more insistent with each failure of a predicted visitation to occur, and even stayed together for several years after the appointed time for the earth's destruction had come and gone. The point is that the godlike Sananda, and the alien world he represented, seemed real and plausible to several other people, sufficiently so that they abandoned their life styles and property in anticipation of being whisked away from the crumbling earth in flying saucers.

The "War of the Worlds" broadcast came in the ambiguously tense time just before America's entry into WWII. It recast H. G. Wells' original book in the present, presented in replicas of on-the-spot radio news coverage. Those who listened heard a reporter describe the disembarkation of a huge, spider-like creature from a cylinder that had fallen to the ground in Grover's Mill, New Jersey, followed by the destruction of New York by invincible tripod war machines. Many listeners, all too predisposed by a real threat of destruction not yet recognized, abandoned their

---

[9] Festinger, Leon, Riecken, Henry W., and Schachter, Stanley. *When Prophecy Fails*. New York: Harper & Row, 1964.

homes and fled from the invasion. Apparently it touched something in them that made it seem vividly real.

I realize it is reckless to assert that "Flash Gordon," specifically the original 1934 movie serial with Buster Crabbe and Charles Middleton, is an invaluable document on the unconscious life of that time. Yet it pertains not only to the relatively harmless UFO phenomenon, but to the profoundly lethal one of National Socialism. It reflects a period when Americans expected a rapprochement with Nazi Germany, and thought of the depression rather than Germany as the paramount threat. German-American groups, holding their swastika rallies on Sunday afternoons, dotted the Middle West. America was open to a small taste of the intrapsychic life of Nazism, and got it from Flash Gordon.

Flash is an all-American blond WASP football hero, or would be, except for his lack of fun and harmless mischief of that stereotype; his face is dour and expressionless. He is coming home from college to visit his father, a famous astronomer, who is studying an alien planet, Mongol, as it nears the earth on collision course. In the midst of the social and meteorological disorder caused by the threatening planet, Flash's plane crashes near the take-off site of Professor Zarkov's rocket ship, so Flash, his girlfriend, and Zarkov take off for planet Mongol together.

Arrival on Mongol, and a change of costume, transform Flash into a sort of heroic, epic character: Siegfried with a liberal dose of Parsifal mixed in. Zarkov emerges as the perennial dwarf-wizard, who continually fashions wonderous implements for Flash to use, even making him invisible at one point, as the dwarf Alberich did for Siegfried. They find the trajectory of the planet under the control of its evil emperor, Ming, the inscrutable stereotype of a Mongolian tyrant. His planet is dying and about to explode, so he needs to conquer and colonize the earth (i.e., to possess it). There is an undeniable linkage between the Asiatic Ming, and one salient aspect of the Nazi propaganda fantasy about the Jews, imputing Asiatic characteristics to them.

But it is not only a collective representation of the shadow that they find; other archaic personages are trapped on Mongol (of course, since a pathogenic complex draws off libido from elsewhere). There is a captive prince from another planet, who closely

98

resembles Wotan, and several others who, more than anything else, resemble the warlike protagonists of Nordic mythology. Flash and Zarkov team up with these, and Ming is finally forced to immolate himself in the subterranean fires of the planet, which were also the power source of the machinery that impelled it toward earth.

Its low comedy aspects aside, Flash Gordon is at an immature level, what *Fidelio* is at a mature one. In the beginning there is a tense relationship with the shadow, and a personal transformation that comes with its resolution and depotentiation. The teaming up with captive alien personages is establishment of an harmonious relationship with the forces of the collective unconscious. Since it takes place at an immature level (and was aimed at preadolescent boys), the anima is handled in a relatively undifferentiated way. The earthly girlfriend is a nonentity, and is held prisoner by Ming during most of the action, and there is a princess (Ming's daughter) who at first tries to vamp Flash, but later helps him (i.e., as the anima becomes more differentiated, she becomes less identified with the shadow).

Summing up, our three examples about outer space show the *concretization of intrapsychic processes* through projection. They ranged from minor to trivial in their effect. But the same course of events can, under the right conditions, take place on a large scale with historic results, as was the case with the Nazi phenomenon.

## JUNG AND THE NAZIS

The problem of Jung's relations with the Nazis is greatly simplified if we consider a passage, written in 1918, containing the elements of the attitude toward the Germans and the Jews, consistently expressed by Jung before, during, and after the Nazi era[10]:

---

[10] Jung himself documented the consistency of these views over the years in "Epilogue to *Essays on Contemporary Events*," (C. W., vol. 10, pars. 458-487), in 1946. I shall refrain from treating this point further, except to say that I have checked the references against the originals, and found them correct.

Christianity split the Germanic barbarian into an upper and lower half, and enabled him, by repressing the dark side, to domesticate the brighter half and fit it for civilization. But the lower, darker half still awaits redemption and a second spell of domestication. Until then, it will remain associated with the vestiges of the prehistoric age, with the collective unconscious, which is subject to a peculiar and ever-increasing activation. As the Christian view of the world loses its authority, the more menacingly will the "blond beast" be heard prowling about in its underground prison, ready at any moment to burst out with devastating consequences. When this happens in the individual it brings about a psychological revolution, but it can also take a social form.

In my opinion, this problem does not exist for the Jews. The Jew already had the culture of the ancient world and on top of that has taken over the culture of the nations amongst whom he dwells. He has two cultures, paradoxical as that may sound. He is domesticated to a higher degree than we are, but he is badly at a loss for that quality in man which roots him to the earth and draws new strength from below. This chthonic quality is found in dangerous concentration in the Germanic peoples.[11]

In view of what later happened, the counterposition of Jews and Germans is as significant as the content of the passage. Our contention was that the principal precondition for the mass eruption of whatever the "underground prison" contains is an atmosphere of threat, against which the individual has no realistic defense. More than enough factors of that description were soon to be operating in Germany. The Germans were disillusioned in WWI, frightened by Red revolutionaries, beleaguered by economic inflation, and then by the great depression. They had enjoyed political unity and colonial self-assertion for a shorter time, and less intensively, than other comparable peoples. In the midst of swift social change and an explosion of new artistic forms, the country seemed to be breaking down into chaos with very many aspirations and potentialities unfulfilled.

To understand the form the eruption took, we must look at the interaction between the external factors and the intrapsychic

---

[11] C. W., vol. 10, pars. 17-18. "The Role of the Unconscious."

processes. Externally, the Germans found their avenues of development blocked. Intrapsychically, it is the shadow that blocks development. If there is no insight, it follows that a strong shadow projection would take place, "explaining" to the individual the frustration being encountered outside. The assortment of lame arguments blaming every setback the Germans had experienced on the Jews is well known. It is impossible to say how much Jung's melding of the German and Jewish questions was prophetic. (We shall keep those questions separate, deferring the Jewish one until the next section.)

The ability of Hitler to represent a "mana-personality"[12] was as much a result of shadow projection as the hatred of the Jews was. When seen from a certain psychological distance, he conveyed a downright comic inferiority.[13] To an involved person, there was a fascinating paradox between his inferior exterior and the sublime religious experience he could evoke. The discrepancy exactly expressed the Germans' awareness of being a great people getting nowhere, so they could identify with him far better than had he looked like one of the race of supermen he wanted to breed. The unconscious contains the worst in us, but also a universal dimension both far better and far worse than we are. A possessed person can bring it out under the right conditions.

Hitler capitalized on many Germanic versions of archetypal myths (*The Nibelungenlied*, the life of King Henry the Fowler, etc.), and it would be a mistake to blame them for the squalid way they were co-opted. Mythical characters naturally find their echo in us, and a positive relationship to them signals a good relationship of our consciousness to the unconscious. Even the swastika had a long history of occurrence in other cultures, as we would expect of a four-fold figure so constructed as to suggest rotation around a center, indicative of individuation.

Only when people are unconscious of these universal things can they be manipulated by them. Mankind must choose between becoming more conscious of them, or acting them out with

---

[12] See ch. 3.

[13] Jung said, "When I saw him with my own eyes, he suggested a psychic scarecrow (with a broomstick for an outstreched arm) rather than a human being." (C. W., vol. 10, par. 419. "After the Catastrophe.")

dreadful consequences. If the honest religious striving that goes with maturity and individuation is not acknowledged, irrational, quasi-religious enthusiasms must ensue. If one does not assimilate the products of the collective unconscious, one will eventually be possessed by them. Among possessed people, there is little the autonomous individual can do to defend himself, as the possession is infectious, even if one has as much insight as Jung:

> Who would have thought in 1900 that it would be possible thirty years later for such things to happen in Germany as are happening today [1934]? Would you have believed that a whole nation of highly intelligent and cultivated people could be seized by the fascinating power of an archetype? I saw it coming, and I can understand it because I know the power of the collective unconscious. But on the surface it looks simply incredible. Even my personal friends are under that fascination, and when I am in Germany, I believe it myself, I understand it all, I know it has to be as it is. One cannot resist it. It gets you below the belt and not in your mind, your brain just counts for nothing, your sympathetic system is gripped. . . . I know highly educated Germans who were just as reasonable as I think I am or as you think you are. But a wave went over them and just washed their reason away, and when you talk to them you have to admit that they could do nothing about it.[14]

Understanding a thing does not necessarily imply ability to deal with it practically, and the topic of Jung's own relationship with the Nazi regime has generated more heat than light until recently. All during the Hitler period, Jung tried to maintain a posture of expedient neutrality, as is generally the custom of the Swiss, and tried to help his colleagues in Germany, and medical psychology generally, to conserve their deteriorating position. In some instances he was effective, but by 1940 he had managed to make himself a pariah to both the Nazis and the Jewish Freudian analysts.

Jung's involvement began in 1933, when he accepted the presidency of the General Medical Society for Psychotherapy, in order to enable it to continue to operate in spite of Nazi restrictions. (Ernst Kretschmer had been his predecessor.) Jung

---

14 Op. cit., Analytical Psychology. . . ., pp. 183-184.

reorganized it along international lines, each country having its own national chapter. Dr. M. H. Göring, a relative of Hermann Göring, became head of the German chapter, the largest of the national chapters. Jung set about making an accommodation with him, so that the Society's journal, the *Zentralblatt für Psychotherapie*, could continue to appear. An issue under Jung's editorship came out in December, 1933. According to the accommodation, the Germans were to print it just as Jung had set it up, ideologically neutral in character, and a supplement, edited by Göring, was to be prepared for distribution in Germany only. Without Jung's knowledge, the journal was released by Göring, including an obnoxious statement about the German members having read *Mein Kampf* "with scholarly seriousness, and accepted it as fundamental." This acutely embarassed Jung, and prompted a good deal of unfair criticism.

In the same number of the *Zentralblatt*, Jung published a controversial article which we will take up in the next section. In the next number, he included an unbound fly-leaf, announcing reorganization of the Society so that membership in it was possible without membership in a national chapter.[15] This made it possible for Jewish psychiatrists who had been expelled from the German chapter to remain as members.[16]

There continued to be pushing and pulling between pro-Axis and anti-Axis factions in the Society until 1939, when Jung resigned because pressure to have the "Aryan" regulations apply to it, became too great. In the preceding six years, Jung had used his position, both publicly and privately, in behalf of many victims of Nazi persecution. In 1940, his name was placed on the Nazi blacklist, and most of his writings were suppressed in Germany. It must be said that in spite of the Nazis' early attempts to win him over, and bring his prestige to the service of their cause, Jung never aligned himself with National Socialism.[17]

---

[15] C. W., vol. 10, pars. 1035-1038.

[16] Dr. Werner Engel of New York tells me this fly-leaf was systematically removed from library copies in a number of countries by Nazis. Obviously the journal made a much different impression with it than without it.

[17] Three important non-Jungian sources that come to that conclusion are Brome (*Op. cit.*, p. 149), Ellenberger (*Op. cit.*, pp. 675-677), and Harms (Ernest, "Carl Gustav Jung—Defender of Freud and the Jews," *Psychiatric Quarterly*, XX(1946), pp. 198-230.

There is a factor besides the practicality of it, that accounts for Jung's failure to align himself more definitely against the Nazi cause. He was generally optimistic about man, and thought the evil in him would not go to extremes without being counter-balanced by its corrective opposite. Just as he thought therapy patients would always throw off spurious, manipulative interpretations in the end, he thought the Germans would recoil from implementing the more venomous aspects of the Nazi platform. In his old age, he criticized himself for having been too optimistic.[18] He said in a letter:

> . . . I really had not thought that man could be so absolutely bad. I thought he could be evil, but evil has at least a certain character, while evil in Germany was rotten. It was a carrion of evil, unimaginably worse than the normal devil. Since Germany is not on the moon, I have drawn my conclusions for the rest of mankind.[19]

## JUNG AND THE JEWS

Our analysis of Jung's relations with the Nazis does not show us the source of the recriminations of pro-Nazi and anti-Jewish sentiment that have persistently been made against him. These have their origin in the more complex problem of his relationship with Judaism and the Jews.

We got a taste of Jung's early view of the Jews in the quote that began the last section. He stated the same view in more detail in that fateful 1934 edition of the *Zentralblatt*, including the most controversial passage in all his work:

> . . . As a member of a race with a three-thousand-year-old civil-ization, the Jew, like the cultured Chinese, has a wider area of psychological consciousness than we. Consequently it is *in general* less dangerous for the Jew to put a negative value on his unconscious.[20] The "Aryan" unconscious, on the other hand, contains explosive forces and seeds of a future yet to be born. . . . The still youthful Germanic peoples are fully capable of creating new cultural forms that still lie dormant

---

[18] Personal communication, Dr. M.-L. von Franz.
[19] To Eugene H. Henley, April 20, 1946. (*Op. cit., C. G. Jung: Letters.*)
[20] He refers to the view of the unconscious expressed by both Freud and Adler, in which the unconscious contains only repressed immoral impulses.

in the darkness of the unconscious of every individual—seeds bursting with energy and capable of mighty expansion. The Jew, who is something of a nomad, has never yet created a cultural form of his own and as far as we can see never will, since all his instincts and talents require a more or less civilized nation to act as host for their development.

The Jewish race as a whole—at least this is my experience—possesses an unconscious which can be compared with the "Aryan" only with reserve. Creative individuals apart, the average Jew is far too conscious and differentiated to go about pregnant with the tensions of unborn futures. The "Aryan" unconscious has a higher potential than the Jewish; that is both the advantage and the disadvantage of a youthfulness not yet fully weaned from barbarism. In my opinion it has been a grave error in medical psychology up till now to apply Jewish categories—which are not even binding on all Jews—indiscriminately to Germanic and Slavic Christendom. Because of this the most precious secret of the Germanic peoples—their creative and intuitive depth of soul—has been explained as a morass of banal infantilism, while my own warning voice has for decades been suspected of anti-Semitism [italics in original].[21]

There is a good deal more to these rather strangely expressed views than meets the eye. While the passage certainly conveys an incorrect and unfair stereotype of the Jews, it stops well short of defaming them. Its basic thesis is that members of cultures with long histories are on such familiar terms with the unconscious that they do not experience it as a spring of creativity and mystery, as members of a newer culture would. Because Freud's psychology reflects such a bias, Jung labelled it a "Jewish psychology," correctly identifying one of its limitations. It is the vicissitudes of belonging to an old, refined culture, and being scattered over many different countries, in them but not really of them, that Jung meant by "Jewish psychology." He was not referring to racial characteristics (his views on which we will come to presently).

While not anti-Semitic, Jung's statements were certainly unclear, and I think it fair to criticize him for what could be thought to be convenient ambiguity under the circumstances. That he himself knew what he was saying is demonstrated by these ex-

---

[21] C. W., vol. 10, pars. 353-354. "The State of Psychotherapy Today."

tracts from letters he wrote in reply to enquiries about the *Zentral-blatt* article:

> As to my assertion that the Jews have not created a "cultural form" of their own, please note that I did not say "culture." I expressly stated that the Jews have a culture nearly 3,000 years old, but one can have a culture without possessing a cultural form of one's own. For instance, Switzerland has a culture but no cultural form."[22]
>
> A people with no ties to the soil, having neither land nor homeland, is commonly called nomadic."[23]

His position did reflect an ignorance of, and insensitivity to things Jewish, which he later took pains to correct.[24] Ironically, Freud and the other Jewish psychoanalysts, with their materialistic attitude and preoccupation with debunking the spiritual side of man, were largely to blame. Freud had said, "We Jews have an easier time, having no mystical element."[25] Indeed, Jung had not had much experience with other Jews, who most certainly do have a mystical element. An improvement of his knowledge about Judaism is shown in a letter to Dr. Göring, of all people:

> Dr. Maier has drawn my attention to your short review of [Alfred] Rosenberg's book [*Der Mythus des zwanzigsten Jahrhunderts*]. For anyone who knows Jewish history, and in particular Hasidism, Rosenberg's assertion that the Jews despise mysticism is a highly regrettable error. I would therefore suggest that we pass over this book in silence.[26]

Several factors worked to worsen the consternation these views caused. Since Jung's work never has been widely understood, few could put his comments, ambiguous or otherwise, into context. An influential Jewish periodical seized on the comparison of the Jews with the Chinese, which, considering Jung's high regard for Chinese culture, was a high compliment, and complained that he had said the Jews were like a "Mongolian horde." Many Freudians

---

[22] To Dr. Gerhard Adler, June 9, 1934 (*Op. cit., C. G. Jung: Letters.*)

[23] To C. E. Bandra, June 19, 1934 (*Ibid.*).

[24] He admitted this in a letter to Dr. B. Cohen, dated March 26, 1934 (*Ibid.*)

[25] Jones, *Op. cit.,* p. 49.

[26] November 16, 1937 (*Op. cit., C. G. Jung: Letters.*)

interpreted his entire creative career as an Oedipal transference with Freud, Jung having created an entire psychology, obviously wrong because it contradicted Freud's, and become anti-Semitic, as an unconscious expression of repressed anti-father hostility. Also, as we have pointed out, Jung always did have a bone to pick with socialists.

A veritable campaign of recrimination began with a letter by Dr. Gustav Bally in the Neue Zürcher,[27] written in response to the Zentralblatt article. It excoriated Jung for the statements his name had been associated with against his will, and falsely accused him of rating the work of Jewish psychologists inferior to that of Gentile ones. Jung rebutted the letter in two later editions of the same paper, stating he had acted as he did because in Germany ". . . a single stroke of the pen would have sufficed to sweep away all psychotherapy,"[28] and criticizing Nazi and other kinds of totalitarianism for all to read.[29] This did not stop the campaign, and a reasonably impartial non-Jungian described the subsequent events: "The campaign originated in Swiss socialist circles, with Theodor Schwarz and Alex von Muralt; it then extended to certain Jewish periodicals, and was renewed a few years later by a small group of psychoanalysts."[30] A number of people carried on such a campaign in the U.S., including Dr. Clara Thompson, then the Executive Director of the Willian Alanson White Foundation.[31]

As far as I can find out, nobody well enough acquainted with Jung to speak with authority about his personal opinions ever joined in making these accusations. Throughout those years, he continued to have close associates who were Jews, including Erich Neumann, Aniela Jaffé, Gerhard Adler, and Jolande Jacobi. None of them reported observing any signs of anti-Semitism on his part.[32]

---

[27] February 27, 1934 (343), Morgenausgabe. A translation of this is included below as Appendix 2. Jung's rejoinder (see below) is part of the Collected Works, but the letter itself has not been accessible in English.

[28] C. W., vol. 10, par. 1017. "A Rejoinder to Dr. Bally."

[29] Ibid., pars. 1016-1035.

[30] Op. cit., Ellenberger, p. 740n.

[31] See Brome (Op. cit., p. 149).

[32] See "C. G. Jung and Nationalism," by Aniela Jaffé (Op. cit., From the Life and Work of C. G. Jung).

Summing up, it was the assertion that there was such a thing as a "Jewish psychology" that prompted most of the controversy. It was fashionable in those days to view man as highly plastic, and governed by a small number of simple principles, like inanimate bodies in Newtonian physics. Cultural traditions were thought of as a superficial acquisition, and an obstacle to social change and the assimilation of people to new social forms. Intellectuals wanted to leave their cultural traditions behind and enter a new age of universal rationality and technology. To stress cultural specificity was to uphold unjust caste and class distinctions, and even superstition. Behaviorism, Freudian psychoanalysis, and socialism shared this system of assumptions in common.

Such one-sidedly relative views have been called "the myth of the universal man"[33] by Jean Paul Sartre, who parallels Jung by recommending choosing oneself as, and authentically being, whatever one is. He expresses the paradox of views in a way that is also implicit in Jung:

> The democrat, like the scientist, fails to see the particular case; to him the individual is only an ensemble of universal traits. It follows that his defense of the Jew saves the latter as a man and annihilates him as Jew. . . . Taking this point of view, he fears the awakening of a "Jewish consciousness" in the Jew; that is, he fears that the Jew will acquire a consciousness of the Jewish collectivity—just as he fears that a "class consciousness" may awaken in the worker. His defense is to persuade individuals that they exist in an isolated state. "There are no Jews," he says, "there is no Jewish question." This means that he wants to separate the Jew from his religion, from his family, from his ethnic community, in order to plunge him into the democratic crucible whence he will emerge naked and alone, an individual and solitary particle like the other particles.

> This is what, in the United States, is called the policy of assimilation; immigration laws have registered the failure of this policy and, on the whole, the failure of the democratic point of view. How could it be otherwise? For a Jew, conscious and proud of being Jewish, asserting his claim to be a member of the Jewish community without ignoring on that

---

[33] Sartre, Jean Paul. *Anti-Semite and Jew.* New York, Schocken, 1948. p. 136.

account the bonds which unite him to the national community, there may not be so much difference between the anti-Semite and the democrat. The former wishes to destroy him as a man and leave nothing in him but the Jew, the pariah, the untouchable; the latter wishes to destroy him as a Jew and leave nothing in him but the man, the abstract and universal subject of the rights of man and the rights of the citizen [my italics].[34]

Such views went down far less easily then than today. Jung was far ahead of his time in seeing there is truth and virtue in having a Jewish, a Germanic, a Chinese, or a Black psychology. What Jung said about the Jews agrees very well with the viewpoint of the Zionists[35] and I am sure he would heartily agree that "Black is beautiful." Man has universal attributes, and needing his particular background and heritage as a point of reference is one of them.

## JUNG, INDIANS, AND BLACK PEOPLE

Implicit in all Jung's discussions of the collective unconscious is the supposition that it is the same for all mankind, that it has to be, for members of one group to be able to respond and relate to another group's culture.

He thought a human life included a built-in destiny needing to unfold, and it is at least plausible that culture and race would be part of that destiny's character. Yet he also saw how the racial and cultural character of a person's psyche could be influenced early in life, in a way not clearly related to the actualization of the Self:

I remember a New York family of German immigrants of which three of the children were born in Germany and four in America. The latter were unmistakably Americans, the first three were clearly Germans. To a keen European eye there is an indefinable yet undeniable something in the whole makeup of the born American that distinguishes him from the born European. It is not so much in the anatomical features as in the general behavior, physical and mental. One

[34] Ibid., pp. 56-57.
[35] As Ellenberger (Op. cit., p. 677.) also points out.

finds it in the language, the gestures, the mentality, in the movements of the body, and in certain things even more subtle than that.[36]

He thought physiognomy was influenced in the same way:

> The greatest experiment in the transplantation of a race in modern times was the colonization of the North American continent by a predominately Germanic population. As the climatic conditions vary very widely, we would expect all sorts of variations of the original racial type. The admixture of Indian blood is increasingly small, so it plays no role. Boas has shown that anatomical changes begin already in the second generation of immigrants, chiefly in the measurements of the skull. At all events the "Yankee" type is formed, and this is so similar to the Indian type that on my first visit to the Middle West,[37] while watching a stream of workers coming out of a factory, I remarked to my companion that I should never have thought there was such a high percentage of Indian blood. He answered, laughing, that he was willing to bet that in all these hundreds of men there would not be found a drop of Indian blood. That was many years ago when I had no notion of the mysterious Indianization of the American people. I got to know of this mystery only when I had to treat many American patients analytically. Remarkable differences were revealed in comparison with Europeans.[38]

We see that far from emphasizing hereditary racial differences, Jung thought environment had more to do with an individual's psychology than heredity. That is an unexpected turn, in thoughts that have generally been too nativistic for the tastes of American psychologists. Surroundings enduringly activate potentialities in the collective unconscious during one's upbringing, in a way not unlike the temporary activation of such potentialities that occurs in psychological contagion. Jung had an experience midway between the two processes, during his trip to East Africa in 1925:

---

[36] C. W., vol. 10, par. 949. "The Complications of American Psychology." (Originally published under the title, "Your Negroid and Indian Behavior," Forum, LXXXIII, 1930, 4, pp. 193-199).

[37] The editors of the Collected Works add the footnote, "Sic, but Buffalo, New York is meant. . . ."

[38] C. W., vol. 10, par. 94, "Mind and Earth."

Only once during the entire expedition did I dream of a Negro. His face appeared curiously familiar to me, but I had to reflect a long time before I could determine where I had met him before. Finally it came to me: he had been my barber in Chattanooga, Tennessee! An American Negro. In the dream he was holding a tremendous, red-hot curling iron to my head, intending to make my hair kinky—that is, to give me Negro hair. I could already feel the painful heat, and awoke with a sense of terror.

I took this dream as a warning from the unconscious; it was saying the primitive was a danger to me. At that time I was obviously all too close to going back.[39]

Such is the process whereby a country like America can develop a mulatto culture, even though the proportion of racially mixed individuals in the dominant white population is small. If one is open to such a variety of experiences, living in a mulatto culture is very enriching. If one is closed to them, if one forces them into one's own shadow side, they become the projections that underlie prejudice. The experiences of culturally, but not racially, mixed countries, like the United States and South Africa falling into that trap are well known.

Below the threshold of consciousness the contagion meets with little resistance. Just as the coloured man lives in your cities and even within your houses, so also he lives under your skin, subconsciously. Naturally it works both ways. Just as every Jew has a Christ complex, so every Negro has a white complex and every American a Negro complex. As a rule the coloured man would give anything to change his skin, and the white man hates to admit that he has been touched by the black.[40]

## JUNG AND THE QUESTION OF WOMAN

We have already covered the distinct, qualitative differences Jung found between masculine and feminine psychology, the former mainly characterized by *Logos*, the latter by *Eros*.[41] To

---

[39] *Op. cit., Memories, Dreams, Reflections*, p. 272.
[40] C. W., vol. 10, par. 963. "The Complications of American Psychology."
[41] See ch. 3.

place this idea, as well as the extreme resistance it currently encounters, into perspective, we must point up an important shift in the general intellectual climate since Jung's time.

Specifically, there was a book that was as widely discussed around the turn of the century, as Freud's analysis of the Oedipus complex was about the middle of the century, but has since become obscure. This is *Mutterrecht* (Mother Right) by J. J. Bachofen.[42] It analyzed Sophocles's trilogy, consisting of *Antigone*, *Oedipus at Colonus*, and *King Oedipus*, and offers an interpretation contrasting sharply with Freud's famous work on the last-mentioned of these.

We have already shown that Freud took the idea of incest too literally, and missed the more central concern it points to, the transformation of the personality through the union of opposites. Focussing our attention on Sophocles's trilogy as a whole, we find *King Oedipus* to be the only part containing incest. All three parts, however, are about conflicts of the generations, and paradoxical conflicts of loyalties. Oedipus unknowingly kills his father Laius, and this eventually leads to the suicide of his mother and wife, Jocasta. Oedipus does wrong, yet rights the wrong his parents had done in abandoning him in the first place. Torn by guilt, Oedipus puts his eyes out, and in *Oedipus at Colonus*, we find him exiled by King Creon, in the company of his two daughters (one of whom is Antigone), but estranged from his two sons who are loyal to Creon, and end up in a bitter power struggle against each other. Finally, in *Antigone*, we find Antigone and Creon's son, Haemon, in opposition to Creon.

According to Bachofen, these conflicts all represent a struggle between matriarchal and patriarchal forms of social organization.[43] The matriarchal principle prevails in the prehistory of any culture.

---

[42] An excellent review may be found in Erich Fromm's *The Forgotten Language* (New York: Grove Press, 1957, pp. 196-231).

[43] He proposed this as an historical formula, and the question of its historical validity has taken quite a beating at the hands of historians and anthropologists. I present it as *psychologically* valid, being in no position to judge its historical merits. Those who confuse the two kinds of validity I put in the same category as those who miss out on the meaning of religion, trying to prove the literal existence of God, or searching for the historical Jesus.

Informal ties of affection and blood relationship bind the group together. Since paternity is difficult to establish (and moreover, since promiscuous sex may be so universal that onset of menstruation rather than sex may be identified as the cause of childbirth), individuals are far more conscious of women than of men as important in life.

As the culture grows, so do formal lines of authority with the men as their main proprietors. Where the people in it had been the group's *raison d'être* in the matriarchal stage, with patriarchy come abstract group purposes to which individuals must be subordinated. Loyalty to the established order supersedes ties of affection and blood. Since the men now physically control the women, ascertaining paternity becomes possible, and is considered important. The "rational" *Logos* predominates over "irrational" *Eros*.[44]

A problem arises, that has its origin in the basic opposition of love and power. All the protagonists have their loyalties divided to some extent, even though each is forthrightly committed to one side or the other. Oedipus is a reactionary, fighting in behalf of the martiarchal. In matriarchal terms he does the right thing (and since the oracle foreordained it, he is in a way not responsible for the result), but by patriarchal standards, killing father and king is the paramount crime. For Jocasta, to abandon her son was the ultimate matriarchal crime against a blood tie; yet she did her duty to the formal obligations of marriage and state, and it would have been equally criminal in its own way for her to ignore it. Haemon and Antigone get caught in the same dilemma in their fight with Creon who, though the ostensive victor, closes the trilogy whimpering about the sterility and spiritual poverty of his own regime.

It would seem that people were still able to see the two principles in perspective early in the industrial revolution, but later became so completely channeled along patriarchal lines that that ability was spoiled. Pulling up roots from the land, becoming

---

[44] The matriarchal principle corresponds to Tönnies definition of community (*Gemeinschaft*), and the patriarchal, to society (*Gesellschaft*). Tönnies, however, saw the transition as smooth, rather than fraught with conflict as Bachofen saw it.

concerned with new problems of technology and administration, and altering society and ourselves to meet those problems, pushed the patriarchal principle into the foreground like nothing ever before. The Freudian emphasis on masculinity, and the concomitant reduction of feminine psychology to penis envy, are representative of an extreme, one-sided patriarchal view of things, and were ahead of their time, coming as they did when the educated people were talking about *Mutterrecht*.

Since Jung was mainly active when intellectuals were talking about Freud and the Oedipus complex, he was ahead of his time too. After him has come a time when men are trying to rediscover their feminine side, and both sexes articulate their longing to rediscover love. The extreme opposite of Freud's penis envy would be womb envy, or pregnancy envy. That theme has occurred in any number of primitive religions, been described by Fromm,[45] and recently revived for popular consumption by Norman Mailer.[46] A psychology reducing masculinity to a compensation for thwarted nurturant impulses is thinkable, although I hope the reaction will not be that extreme.

Summing up, we have characterized masculine and feminine psychology, each being present in every individual, helping to account for the marvelous inconsistency of human nature. Each must integrate the other-sex component within, for the individual personality to develop. Since the era from which we are now passing stifled and devalued the feminine, we would expect to find that men were made sick, and women, even sicker, as a result. The current cacophony of discussion about the rôles of the sexes confirms that expectation.

At the risk of offending some radical feminists, I have seen very little to contradict Jung's description of feminine psychology:

> ... by taking up a masculine profession, studying and working like a man, woman is doing something not wholly in accord with, if not directly injurious to, her feminine nature. . . . I do not mean merely physiological injury but above all psychic injury. It is a woman's outstanding characteristic that she can do anything for the love of a man. But those women who

---
[45] *Ibid.*, p. 233.
[46] "The Prisoner of Sex." *Harper's Magazine*, vol. 242 (1450), March, 1971, p. 41ff.

can achieve something important for the love of a *thing* are most exceptional, because this does not really agree with their nature. Love for a thing is a man's prerogative. But since masculine and feminine elements are united in our human nature, a man can live in the feminine part of himself, and a woman in her masculine part. Nonetheless the feminine element in man is only something in the background, as is the masculine element in woman. If one lives out the opposite sex in oneself one is living in one's own background, and one's real individuality suffers. . . . The contrasexual element in either sex is always dangerously close to the unconscious [italics in original].[47]

He said it a little differently in a letter:

We know very well that a man's ambition is for his concepts to be realized in life, whereas it is the most secret longing of all women for their lives to be realized in concepts. This is not a fundamental criticism, only a friendly hint at the very natural fact that a man wants to understand, whereas a woman wants to be understood. For this purpose she tries to make her life understandable to herself.[48]

In spite of the built-in, constitutional tendency to the contrary, we observe women eager to be just like men in the patriarchal order, just as we observe men submerging their individuality in mass ideologies. How is it possible for women to be pushed so far into their inferior masculine aspect that they become completely animus-possessed?

This is abetted by woman's own unconsciousness and passivity, useful though these may be from the biological point of view: she allows herself to be convinced by the man's projected feelings. Of course this is a general human characteristic, but in a woman it is given a particularly dangerous twist, because in this respect she is not naïve and it is only too often her *intention* to let herself be convinced by them. It fits in with her nature to keep her ego and her will in the background, so as not to hinder the man in any way, and to invite him to realize his intentions with regard to her person. This is a sexual pattern, but it has far-reaching ramifications in the feminine psyche. By maintaining a passive attitude with an

---

[47] C. W., vol. 10, par. 243. "Woman in Europe."
[48] To Miss C. Kaufmann, March 12, 1934 (*Op. cit.*, *C. G. Jung: Letters.*).

ulterior purpose, she helps the man to realize his ends and in that way holds him. At the same time she is caught in her own toils, for whoever digs a pit for others falls into it himself [italics in original].[49]

To be sure, this does not mean that women should be discriminated against in occupations and professions, or restricted to *Küche, Kinder, und Kirche.* We find vital, unneurotic women in almost every walk of life, whose secret is the inclusion of a humane, feminine objective and style in what they do. It is one thing to integrate the animus, and another to be possessed by him, so that the individual personality and the indispensable feeling-relatedness to others suffer. Jung summed it up facetiously, "a woman's place is on the weak side of a man."[50]

## JUNG AND THE DILEMMA OF MODERN LIFE

Jung kept himself relatively aloof from the materialistic concerns and popular culture that make up the life style of urban people in our time. Working in his house in Küsnacht, he was in, but not of industralized Switzerland. He preferred being at his tower in Bollingen, where the distractions of telephone and radio, and even the electric light were excluded. Constant exposure to these, he thought, caused a distortion of the individual personality in favor of extraversion, and estrangement from one's inner roots. He rarely mentioned the problem, but his position is clearly expressed in a letter:

> . . . noise is certainly only one of the evils of our time, perhaps the most obtrusive. The others are the gramophone, the radio, and now the blight of television. I was once asked by an organization of teachers, why, in spite of the better food in elementary schools, the curriculum could no longer be completed nowadays. The answer is: lack of concentration, too many distractions. When children do their work to the accompaniment of the radio, so much is fed into them from outside that they no longer have to think of something they could be doing from inside themselves, which requires

---

[49] C. W., vol. 10, par. 240. "Woman in Europe."
[50] C. W., vol 9¹, par. 440. "The Phenomenology of the Spirit in Fairy-tales."

concentration. Their infantile dependence on the outside is thereby increased and prolonged into later life where it becomes fixed in the well known attitude that every inconvenience should be abolished by order of the state. . . . This is the degenerative symptom of urban civilization, to which we must now add the nerve-shattering din of our technological gadgetry. The alarming pollution of our water supplies, the steady increase of radioactivity and the somber threat of over-population with its genocidal tendencies have already led to a widespread though not thoroughly conscious fear which loves noise because it stops the fear from being heard. Noise is welcome because it drowns the inner instinct of warning [italics in original].[51]

This forced extraversion is no minor irritation. We have shown that one must assimilate the activity of the unconscious, because its dissociation leads to invasion; to autonomous manifestation of the unconscious either through neurotic symptoms, or some sort of blind acting-out behavior. Also, the conscious life will be very dull, soulless and lacking in spirit, if the conscious attitude is alienated. No matter how exciting external circumstances may be, the vitality with which to respond productively to them can come only from the unconscious.

Interference with the natural tendency to introversion is particularly undesirable for children, whose development involves fantasy, interspersed with the withdrawal of fantastic projections ("it was only my imagination"). The traditional fairy tales every culture produces are a collective vehicle for this process, and have a constant form expressive of universal human strivings.[52]

I have had several acquaintances who, going along with current fashions in child rearing, thought they should shield their small children from traditional fairy tales, lest the children follow the examples of violence and immorality often depicted in them. When the parents did read old fairy tales to the children (because I cajoled them into it), they were usually surprised how well the

---

[51] To Prof. Karl Oftinger, September, 1957 (*Op. cit.*, *C. G. Jung: Letters.*)
[52] See C. W., vol. 9,[1] pars. 384-455. "The Phenomonology of the Spirit in Fairy Tales." Also, vol. 17, pars. 127-229. "Analytical Psychology and Education." Dr. von Franz takes up the content of fairy tales in *Interpretation of Fairy Tales* (New York: Spring Publications, 1970), and *The Feminine in Fairy Tales* (New York: Spring Publications, 1972).

children differentiated the symbolic violence from real violence, and related to the tales without any interpretation being necessary. Encouragement of the imagination of children aids in establishing a balance between the collective unconscious and the conscious personality, and hopefully reduces the likelihood of dangerous manifestations of the former, later in life.

The famous sociologist, David Riesman, reached practically the same conclusion in *The Lonely Crowd*.[53] He pointed out the popular children's story, *Tootle the Engine*, as a prime example of an attempt to contrive and prefabricate fantasy, and thereby estrange it from unconscious life. Tootle is a little steam locomotive who nearly spoils his chances for upward mobility by going off the tracks to smell the flowers. His peers, after some difficulty, succeed in teaching him that he must always stay on the tracks and obey the signals if he wants to grow up to be a streamliner. There is nothing to it but a propaganda message of conformity.

Reiman contrasts this with the traditional fairy tale, "Little Red Riding Hood." Superfically, it too seems to be designed to caution children into obedience. But on a deeper level (that Tootle lacks because he is only made out of pot iron), the story deals with the universal concerns of sexual temptation and defloration (hence the multiple symbolism of the story's title). The contamination of sexuality with aggression, symbolized by the wolf that devours Red Riding Hood and her grandmother, is a typical problem of immaturity. Fromm stresses that the wolf alternately impersonates Red Riding Hood and her grandmother, and by putting them in his belly, makes a ludicrous attempt at usurping the matriarchal rôle.[54] So, the story is also about pregnancy envy.

Most of the questions people have about the quality of modern life are bound up with the transition from Red Riding Hood to Tootle. Jung was optimistic about the ultimate response to that transition:

> I know a case in my own experience where children who have been brought up in a too rationalistic way, that is have been deprived of a proper knowledge of the fairy world, have

---

[53] New Haven: Yale University Press, 1961, pp. 104-107.
[54] *Op. cit.*, pp. 235-241.

invented fairy tales all by themselves, obviously to fill the gap
left by the stupid prejudices of the adults.[55]

## JUNG AND PSYCHEDELIC DRUGS

One good thing about the explosion in the use of hallucinogenic
drugs in the sixties was its confrontation of the behavioral science
establishment with intrapsychic contents that no amount of
analysis of the individual's past experiences could explain. *Tabula
rasa* psychologists and symbolic interactionist sociologists are
forced to respond to student questions about drug experiences,
that their models don't account for them. Accordingly, I have
seen the typical professorial reaction to comments on the collective unconscious change from rejection of it out of hand as a
preposterous notion, to passing over it in fairly respectful silence.
Since dreams demonstrate, quite as satisfactorily as drug trips,
the operation of an impersonal, unlearned psychic substrate in
each of us, those to whom the findings with psychedelic drugs
came as a surprise, must have been looking at the human experience in a very one-sided way.

If only because the material reported by the LSD experimenters
resembles the dreams and drawings of Jung's more fluent patients,
the temptation to insinuate Jung into claims that an effortless and
instantaneous royal road to the unconscious has been found is
strong.[56] Even if he had never known of LSD, we could predict
he would be totally skeptical of any possible benefits from its
use. Even at his most optimistic, he knew that the posture of the
conscious attitude toward the immeasurably greater power of the
unconscious was a touchy matter. And his assessment of the destructive potential was sometimes short of the mark. He did hear
of some early LSD experiments, before anyone ever thought they
would become a major influence in our culture, and commented
on them in a letter:

> I only know there is no point in wishing to know more of
> the collective unconscious than one gets through dreams and

---

[55] Letter to John Symonds, October 13, 1953. (*Op. cit., C. G. Jung: Letters*).

[56] Timothy Leary did so in a popular article that appeared just as this
section was being written ("The Principles & Practice of Hedonic Psychology," *Psychology Today*, vol. 6(8), January, 1973, pp. 52-58).

instruction. The more you know of it, the greater and heavier becomes your moral burden, because the unconscious contents transform themselves into your individual tasks and duties as soon as they begin to become conscious. Do you want to increase loneliness and misunderstanding? Do you want to find more and more complications and increasing responsibilities? You get enough of it. If I once could say that I had done everything I know I had to do, then perhaps I should realize a legitimate need to take mescalin. But if I should take it now, I would not be sure at all that I had not taken it out of idle curiosity. I should hate the thought that I had touched on the sphere where the paint is made that colours the world, where the light is created that makes shine the splendour of the dawn, the lines and shapes of all form, the sound that fills the orbit, the thought that illuminates the darkness of the void. There are some poor impoverished creatures, perhaps, for whom mescalin would be a heavensent gift without a counterpoison, but I am profoundly mistrustful of the "pure gifts of the Gods." You pay dearly for them.

It is quite awful that the alienists have caught hold of a new poison to play with, without the faintest knowledge or feeling of responsibility. It is as if the surgeon had never learned further than to cut open the patient's belly and to leave things there [italics in original].[57]

These diverse topics serve to show us the destructive implications of the collective unconscious, in contrast to the healing ones shown in chapter 3. They bring us to the central premise of Jung's psychology, recognition of greater maturity of consciousness as the most important human concern. That is easier to say than to achieve, since it touches every part of the human enigma. In our culture, it means elevating spiritual development as a priority. (In a country like India, far ahead of us in developing man's inner resources, perhaps out of necessity because the external facts of life there are so grim, extraverted accomplishment is the inferior side needing to be developed.) For us, according to Dr. von Franz, "The only adventure that is still worthwhile . . . lies in the inner realm of the unconscious psyche."[58]

[57] To Father Victor White, April 10, 1954 (Op. cit., C. G. Jung: Letters). Jung was not familiar with the chemistry of LSD, and thought it the same as mescalin.
[58] Op. cit., Man and His Symbols, p. 211.

# CHAPTER 6

# Jung and Academic Psychology

"We have become rich in knowledge, but poor in wisdom." (C. W., vol. 5, par. 23, *Symbols of Transformation.*

It is truly amazing how little contact there has been between Jung's psychology and the enterprise of academic psychology. Only in part is this due to a basic incompatibility. Jung's psychology is genuinely incommensurable with viewpoints that make psychology (or behavior, if you prefer) a matter of what comes into the individual from outside.

> The disastrous idea that everything comes to the human psyche from outside and that it is born a *tabula rasa* is responsible for the erroneous belief that under normal circumstances the individual is in perfect order. . . . As a result of these prejudices, the individual feels totally dependent on the environment and loses all capacity for introspection. In this way his code of ethics is replaced by a knowledge of what is permitted or forbidden or ordered. How, under these circumstances, can one expect a soldier to subject an order received from a superior to ethical scrutiny? He has not yet made the discovery that he might be capable of spontaneous ethical impulses, and of performing them—even when no one is looking.[1]

Mechanistic determinism and ethical irrelevance, the result of too extraverted an approach, characterize a large portion if not most of academic psychology. It is not surprising that psychologists of that stripe are hopelessly dissociated from Jung. There are,

---

[1] C. W., vol. 9¹, par. 479. "On the Psychology of the Trickster-Figure."

however, some other topics in academic psychology that have a great deal to do with Jung, where formulations that could pass for paraphrases of his work have gained wide acceptance. "Self-actualization" theory and the work of Erich Fromm are important cases in point. More importantly, there is the highly compatible, but differently focused *Gestalt* psychology of Wertheimer, Köhler, and Koffka, that has recently given rise to some new developments. Jung's psychology and *Gestalt* psychology are like two parallel lines that have been moving in the same direction without touching; I contend that psychology will change very much when these alter course a little, and meet.

## "SELF-ACTUALIZATION" THEORY

The idea that a person has an intrinsic, characteristic individuality to assert has come into the mainstream of American academic psychology from a variety of sources,[2] the most popular and best articulated of which is Abraham Maslow. He divides human interests into D (deficiency) cognitions, and B (being) cognitions. D cognition is selective apperception of a thing according to the needs of the cognizer. Such cognition is self-interested, and leads to an exploitive relationship of cognizer to cognizand. B cognition is for the sake of the cognized; it is a selfless striving toward a higher form of order and meaning, rather than a striving to meet a need.

Maslow utilizes a hierarchy of five human motives.[3] The first four, physiological tissue tensions, safety, belongingness and love, and self-esteem are the bases of D cognition. "Self-actualization," the highest human motive, underlies B cognition.

> The multitude of idiosyncratic motives which come under the head of "self-actualization" can hardly be listed since each person has different talents, capacities, potentialities. But some characteristics are general to all of them. And one is that these impulses are desired and welcomed, are enjoyable and

---

[2] Including Carl R. Rogers's *Client Centered Therapy* (Boston: Houghton-Mifflin, 1951), Rollo May's *Man's Search for Himself* (New York: Norton, 1953), Gordon Allport's *Becoming* (New Haven: Yale U. Press, 1955), and Marie Jahoda's *Current Concepts of Positive Mental Health* (New York: Basic Books, 1958).

[3] Maslow, A. H. *Motivation and Personality*, New York: Harpers, 1954.

pleasant, that the person wants more of them rather than less, and that if they constitute tensions, they are *pleasurable* tensions. The creator ordinarily welcomes his creative impulses, the talented person enjoys using and expanding his talents.

It is simply inaccurate to speak in such instances of tension-reduction, implying thereby the getting rid of an annoying state. For these states are not annoying. [italics in original][4]

This "self-actualization" has a decidedly expansionistic temperament. It seems that the B cognizer is always impelled to some kind of productive intercourse with the object of his cognition. One receives the impression that the "self-actualized" person moves restlessly from the old to the new, and that change is the bane of his existence. With Maslow the American ideal of progress becomes the center-piece of a general theory of human nature. A member of a slow changing, traditional culture could not "self-actualize," and would lead something less than a fully satisfying human life, according to him.

Maslow identified Kurt Goldstein, who originally introduced the term, "self-actualization," as his intellectual forerunner.[5] Goldstein was a neurologist who applied *Gestalt* psychology to the diagnosis of organic impairment, and found such great qualitative distinctions between intact and impaired organisms as to discredit comparisons between organs studied in isolation, and the same organs functioning in the context of a whole, intact organism. Goldstein's "self-actualization" referred to an organism adapting according to its nature, to the environment for which its innate capacities suit it.[6] His view is biological, while Maslow's (like Jung's) is phenomenological. Goldstein is not primarily concerned with individual differences in human personalities. Lower animals are not less "self-actualizing" than man in this sense, while it is the essence of Maslow's view that "self-actualization" is a uniquely human attribute.[7] He explicitly states the opinion that B

---

[4] Maslow, A. H. *Toward A Psychology of Being*. Princeton: D. Van Nostrand, 1962, p. 27.

[5] Maslow dedicated *Toward a Psychology of Being* to Goldstein.

[6] Goldstein, Kurt. *The Organism*. New York: American Book Co., 1939, p. 197.

[7] I am indebted to Dr. Nehemiah Jordan for pointing this out to me.

cognition (and therefore "self-actualization") are not to be found in lower animals.[8] Apparently he was not familiar with experiments on curiosity and manipulative motives in animals, that are described in every General Psychology textbook.

Maslow and Jung both emphasize the self-determining individual unfolding; accordingly, Maslow's viewpoint is much more similar to that of Jung, than to that of Goldstein. Maslow got stuck on a spurious way of distinguishing human from infrahuman psychology, while Jung, with his emphasis on symbolism, found a valid way of doing that. It is ironic that Maslow chose Goldstein as his intellectual father-imago, while making only desultory references in passing to Jung.

## ERICH FROMM

The nearest thing to Jung's approach to achieve wide currency in the United States is found in various books by Erich Fromm. Their clear and readable presentation has opened up many avenues that would otherwise have remained closed in many an undergraduate education, including my own. His *The Forgotten Language* was the only conspicuous open-minded treatment of dream interpretation prior to the popularity of Existential Psychology. His *Escape From Freedom* and *Man For Himself* take almost the same standpoint toward the individual's ambivalent relationship with the collective, as Jung. In *You Shall Be As Gods* and *The Heart of Man*, he wrestles with the same problems that prompted Jung to write *Answer to Job*. One just couldn't look into the effect of Jung's work, and ignore Fromm.

In *The Forgotten Language*,[9] Fromm correctly summarizes Freud's approach to symbolism as disguised repression, and Jung's, as a reflection of something that transcends the individual man. He then sets forth his own approach, explaining symbolism as the expression of the creative individual personality asserting itself, and trying to throw off those influences of waking life that stultify it.[10] He admits to a certain uniformity of those expressions from individual to individual, and from culture to culture, and calls the

---

[8] Op. cit., *Toward a Psychology of Being*, p. 25.
[9] Op. cit.
[10] Ibid., p. 97.

recurring contents "universal symbols." For all practical purposes, he handles his "universal symbols" the same as Jungians handle archetypes. Yet, Fromm rejects the hypothesis of the collective unconscious out of hand, and generally ignores the problems of the origins of the "universal symbols" universality, and the individual personality's individuality. Since Jung's solutions to those problems evoked so much misunderstanding and prejudice, Fromm probably does well to pass over the issues so lightly.

Fromm did not stop at using ideas similar to Jung's to appear more original than he really was, to a readership more or less unfamiliar with Jung. He once quoted a long dream of one of Jung's patients, one of events that took place in a church,[11] that Jung had interpreted as expressive of a not yet realized religious longing of the dreamer, who had an early dogmatic religious education, and was later totally occupied with economic and materialistic concerns. Fromm reinterpreted the dream as signifying incompleteness in the dreamer's emanicpation from religious dogmatism, denying that there could be such a thing as an authentic religious inclination. He accused Jung of forcing his own preconceived ideas onto the dream, something of which he, himself, could more aptly be accused. Jung, after all, had known the dreamer firsthand, while Fromm knew him only through Jung's discreetly incomplete account.

On other topics, I think it is enough to point out that Fromm closely parallels Jung in advocating that the individual be autonomous, rather than neurotic or compliant, toward the collective, and toward ethical questions. While Jung's most forceful and articulate writings in that vein[12] appeared long after Fromm's best known works, the seminal ideas had already appeared in Jung's work by 1920.[13] Fromm claims a thorough knowledge of Jung. The telling truth of the matter is that scarcely anywhere has he a kind word to say about Jung.

---

[11] Ibid., pp. 97-101. He got it from C. W., vol. 11, par. 40. *Psychology and Religion*.

[12] For example, *The Undiscovered Self* (C. W., vol. 10, pars. 488-588).

[13] C. W., vol. 7, pars. 202-406. *The Relations Between the Ego and the Unconscious*, and vol. 6, *Psychological Types*.

## GESTALT PSYCHOLOGY

Many younger psychologists are almost unaware that Gestalt Psychology is not a school of psychotherapy that began in California in the sixties, but an esoteric psychology of perception and cognition that began in Germany before WWI. The rise of Hitler caused the major Gestaltists to relocate in the United States, where their viewpoint failed to take root because it ran counter to the same mechanistic, reductionistic myth that gave rise to behaviorism. The psychologies of consciousness that existed before Gestalt Psychology were based on British associationistic philosophy, and studied mental elements combining to produce complex thoughts, "mental molecules," and the like.[14] The substitution of stimulus and response connections for the earlier mental elements brings us up to the present day in academic psychology.

Whole percepts and concepts, rather than the elements of which they are composed, are the principal objects of study in Gestalt Psychology. Laws of composition of percepts and concepts are the expected outcome. The Gestaltists found a set of such laws governing visual perception, now found in virtually every General Psychology text.[15] We have already noted the affinity of the Gestaltist idea of a perceptual or cognitive field differentiated into a figure and ground, and the Jungian idea that the psyche is a field that becomes lawfully differentiated, giving rise to symbols or archetypes.[16] While it happens that the Gestaltists investigated conscious instances of this process of differentiation, I know of nothing in their work that would exclude Jung's work on the unconscious ones.

Since it has been our contention that a holistic viewpoint (and one not without its teleological overtones) represents life as we find it, more accurately than a reductionistic one does, it is worthwhile to take note of an historical anomaly: Gestalt Psychology is dead in university psychology departments and labora-

---

[14] For an adequate treatment of these developments, I recommend *Seven Psychologies* by Edna Heidbreder (New York: Appleton-Century-Crofts, 1933 and 1961).

[15] But there is a better treatment in Heidbreder (*Ibid.*), pp. 347-351.

[16] See chs. 2 and 3.

tories, but still very much alive in neurological wards and clinics. It was Goldstein who adopted Gestaltism to the latter settings. He found that brain-injured patients, irrespective of the local effects of their injuries, lost what he called the *abstract attitude*: they lost their ability to detach their awareness from present, concrete objects. Only if a new set of stimuli were familiar and concrete, could they make a *Gestalt* of them. The patients could adapt very well to familiar situations, but utilized an effortful attention to details, such as a normal person would not find necessary; whenever concepts had to be applied to unfamiliar situations, they would fail dramatically at coping with them. For example, a severely brain-damaged patient might learn his way around his immediate surroundings in the hospital; if, one day, he got off the elevator on the wrong floor, where the floor plan was the same but the furnishings and details were different, he might then be completely unable to find his way. For Goldstein, this meant that a field of some sort had lost part of its ability to become differentiated.

With this loss of ability to adapt went the experience of loss of part of oneself and part of one's surroundings to awareness. When the abstract attitude is impaired, and concrete relatedness to familiar environs is interrupted, one feels oneself cast into nothingness. Goldstein defined the emotional response to such an erasure of awareness as *anxiety*. In other words, it is the frustration of the single fundamental drive of "self-actualization" that causes anxiety. This is in contradistinction to *fear*, which responds to some particular, explicit danger.[17] Apparently oblivious to the compatibility of his position to Jung's, Goldstein speculated on the implications of his position for Freudianism:

> In the light of our discussion non-conscious phenomena take on a character that is totally different from the one psychoanalysis ascribes to them. We divorce them from their negative denotation as repressed conscious phenomena, charged with the tendency to reoccupy the forbidden grounds of consciousness; indeed, we try to acknowledge them as events of a positive, unartificial, and observable nature. Finally, we attempt to evaluate their significance for and influence upon

---

[17] Goldstein, Kurt. *Human Nature.* New York: Schocken Books, 1963, p. 92.

behavior, be it normal or pathological. With this we avoid the wrong hypostatization of functional (i.e., configurational) events to separate driving forces, which is so characteristic of the Freudian theory; we thereby escape the wrong theory of drives, as well as the false overestimation of single factors which determine life—for example, sex.[18]

Following these suggestions, we find some possible parallels between Goldstein and Jung, besides their mutual emphasis on the one drive of self-actualization (or Self-actualization). It is a part of the general lore of clinical psychology that psychologically disturbed, and particularly, psychotic persons show a decrement in ability to apply the abstract attitude in psychological tests. In Jungian terms, we would say that the balanced interplay between projection and sensory intake, that we identified earlier as the essence of human adaptation, is disturbed. That such disturbance is in fact a key attribute shared in common by organic brain pathology and psychopathology, agrees with the expectations of both viewpoints. (Regulated projection to order reality would correspond to attainment of a *Gestalt*.) A parallel between organically caused distortion of the psychic field, and psychically caused distortion—i.e., dissociation—presents itself. In either case, the interrelatedness of phenomena in the psychic field is disturbed. The correspondence of the views is not perfect, Goldstein's deemphasis of the inner division so important to Jung being one important difference. But from the two taken together, we gain some insight into what future understanding of psychopathology might be like.

Since our rapprochement between the two viewpoints has so far depended on their similar use of "psychic fields" as vehicles for order and meaning, the comparison may seem superficial. The "psychic fields" seem very closely tied to the physiological substrate; Jung departed radically from normal physical conceptions of reality with his principle of synchronicity,[19] and in so doing limited the possible comparability of his standpoint to the primarily physiological one we have, up to this point, portrayed Gestalt Psychology to be. But instead of parting company with

---

[18] *Ibid.*, p. 165.
[19] See ch. 4.

Jung at that juncture, we find that Gestalt Psychology also took a speculative look beyond the space-time-cause-effect view of reality.

Wolfgang Köhler set out to evaluate the implications of modern physics for his scientific but non-positivistic psychology in *The Place of Value in a World of Facts*,[20] much as Jung did in *Synchronicity: An Acausal Connecting Principle*.[21] Köhler was not interested in occult phenomena, and Jung was only incidentally interested in the philosophy of the natural sciences. Yet, the similarity of conclusions to which the two came is striking.

Starting with the desire to handle some of the profound, paradoxical questions that any intelligent child asks, and also the practical problems from which university professors kept themselves strictly aloof in his day, Köhler set out to show that there was some continuity between the psyche and the physical universe. He began by placing distance between himself and what he called the doctrine of "Nothing But." "Nothing But" placed a high value on nature as such, and on "objective" knowledge of it, free from man's distortions and superstitions. This amounts to knowledge of its chance distributions, since inherent order in nature is seen as "Nothing But" a subjective distortion. Because science must deal with isolated aspects of reality, these become the "truth," and one then cannot help but lose one's bearings if enlightenment on basic human issues is sought therein.

> "Many statements by which advancing science makes man and his environment appear discolored and devalued are suspect of being 'correct' statements that are not actually true. . . . They refer to some properties of the world in its relation to man, but preferably to those which are not relevant for the picture of man in his relation to this world and for the knowledge of man himself."[22]
>
> "The main issue, then, is clearly this: Is the human mind to be regarded as a domain of mere indifferent facts? Or do intrinsic demands, fittingness, and its opposite, wrongness, occur among the genuine characteristics of the contents? This question . . . is in principle the same whether we consider the

---

[20] New York: Mentor Books, 1966. The contents originated as the 1934-1935 William James Lectures at Harvard University.

[21] C. W., vol. 8, pars. 816-968.

[22] Op. cit., The Place of Value. . . ., p. 29. This quote and the following one are in quotation marks because they are part of a dialogue in the original.

more intellectual or the moral and the aesthetic phases of mental life."[23]

Central to this discussion is Köhler's notion of "requiredness," the fitness or necessaryness of the structure of phenomena. (The influences of Plato, Kant, and Husserl are evident here.) "There is, phenomenally, something remarkably 'objective' about conceptual truth in so far as its content seems segregated from the stream of thinking. There is, besides, the remarkable difference between the directness of 'evidence' or requiredness on one side and the indirectness of guesses and of verifications of factual laws on the other."[24]

Requiredness is not reducible to habit, striving, or aesthetics, but is a precondition of them. There are three required qualities of Gestalten: 1) They exhibit "definite segregated units or contexts in all degrees of complexity, articulation, and clearness."[25] 2) They are systematic, and participate in their contexts. 3) They have a goal quality, and are purposeful. In this connection, Köhler proceeds from the biological notion of "interest" of Ralph Barton Perry to a discussion of vectors of required behavior further developed in the field theory of Lewin and the self-actualization theory of Goldstein.

Requiredness is the essence of what Köhler means by the term "value." The objective forces organizing a field, which has objective requirements, giving rise to meaning, are its "value." Köhler did not mean the mere evaluation of goals, as the usual use of the term in the social sciences would imply. He expressed no more than a vague intimation of the practical applications of these concepts which were later to come from Lewin and Goldstein.

The phenomena we can know are referred to by Köhler as the "phenomenal world" (also known as the "phenomenal given"). The object of knowledge lies in the transphenomenal realm. This cannot be directly known.

An object sends out messages which stimulate sense organs. Thereupon other messages begin to travel through nerves

[23] Ibid., p. 36.
[24] Ibid., p. 51.
[25] Ibid., p. 75.

toward the brain and, if this brain is functioning normally, a percept emerges. This is a long chain of processes. It is besides, the only functional connection between the percept and the object from which the train of messages first issued. Have we any right, then, to identify the percept at one end of the chain with the object at the other end?[26]

We do, if we make two assumptions:

> First, we should have to assume that the phenomenal world and transphenomenal reality belong to one common realm of existence, in which transposition is possible from one domain to the other. The second condition is that "reference"— generally or at least in some of its forms—be a common functional trait of both phenomenal and transphenomenal existence, more particularly: that a reference may extend from a phenomenal term on the one hand to a transphenomenal term on the other. [italics in original] [27]

So science, which must ultimately depend on the phenomenal realm for what it can know about the transphenomenal, depending often on inferences and indirect "pointer readings," is subjective. Any potential object of scientific study which finds no echo in the "subjective," phenomenal realm will just have to suffer to remain not understood. Köhler intimated that the progress of subatomic physics may ultimately be halted by this difficulty. Even the concepts of self, of location inside and outside the self, and memories (be they traces or something else) are in the phenomenal realm; they are never transcended.

A particularly important quality that the phenomenal and transphenomenal presumably have in common is that they are fields. The elements of a field's microscopic structure are so interrelated that order and segregation of boundaries are exhibited in the macroscopic structure. For perception to be useful, there must be a correspondence between the physical (and the physiological) field and the psychological one. This assumption is the principle of *isomorphism*.

> Continuity is a *structural* trait of the visual field. It is also a *structural* fact that in this field circumscribed particular per-

[26] *Ibid.*, p. 93.
[27] *Ibid.*, p. 97.

cepts are segregrated as patches, figures, and things. In both characteristics, we have found, the macroscopic aspect of cortical processes resembles visual experience. To this extent, therefore, vision and its cortical correlate are *isomorphic*. . . . The fact which mediates between the physical and the perceptual structure is . . . found to be *cortical* organization, which, as a rule, resembles both. [italics in original].[28]

For the same reason that microscopic elements give rise to a macroscopic form which represents a qualitatively different level, mechanistic explanations of biological organisms fail. Köhler described the indefinite series of regulating devices which the process of natural selection would have had to build in, to account for the myriad of specific postures and behaviors that may have a similar meaning and a similar goal. He also noted that organisms do not seek equilibrium (like machines with regulating devices) but rather to function optimally according to their nature. What they are and how they function is a macroscopic problem.

*Requiredness* means that a given context either accepts its own constitution and the nature of its own parts, or that it rejects some phase of this given status. Requiredness is either final and complete, or it demands such changes as would lead to a more completely acceptable state. It may also assume the form of objection to such changes as make requiredness less complete [italics in original].[29]

Köhler illustrated the hiatus between man and "reality" by telling a dream he had during his visit to Harvard University to give the lectures on which *The Place of Value in a World of Facts* is based. At a lecture, someone had called him a materialist because of his preoccupation with physics. In the dream, Köhler is on trial, charged with the offense of being a materialist. To give him a chance to prove otherwise, an old man and a guard accompany him to a forest in Maine, and from there to a strange village via a tunnel. They come to some buildings, one of which is labeled "Department of Physics." Here, they are able to find out nothing about matter; only protons, neutrons, and electrons defined in

---

[28] *Ibid.*, p. 170.
[29] *Ibid.*, p. 263.

terms of one another, and spaces in which they reverberate, are known there. To find out about matter, they are finally referred to the psychology department, since matter (e.g. substantiality) is a percept, and not a result of the microscopic anaylsis of things.

I realize that Köhler's arguments are extremely, perhaps unreasonably hard to follow (as much so in the original as in the present condensed account). Arguments about that which by nature is outside the human purview cannot be otherwise. What Köhler and Jung shared in common is the view that science is ultimately a subjective, human product, that it is an illusion to think that science can ever be totally objective, transcend the human viewpoint, or know its subject matter as it "really" is. Both imply that scientists must reinforce their attitude of tentativity, and learn to tolerate a lot of ambiguity.

Summing up, we have identified three striking similarities between Gestalt Psychology and Jung: 1) The non-positivistic, experiencer-oriented standpoint on the nature of science, just discussed. 2) The choice of psychic wholes (that qualify both as perceptions and cognitions) as the principal objects of study, these wholes being composed in a consistent and lawful way. 3) The understanding of motivation as a single force, broadly characteristic of the type of organism exhibiting it, and subsuming the so-called specific biological and psychological drives. These are remarkable similarities for psychologies that have utterly different content, and developed independently. And their strange relationship does not end there.

## AFTER GESTALT PSYCHOLOGY

There are two important contemporary thinkers who to me seem genuinely in the *Gestalt* tradition, though they, themselves, deny it. These are Michael Polanyi and Arthur Koestler. Perhaps we can speak of a *holistic psychology* that has succeeded Gestalt Psychology, Polanyi and Koestler being its foremost proponents. These contributors enhance the correspondence of holistic psychology to Jung by adding two further topics to the three just stated: 4) The hierarchical organization of systems, living and nonliving. 5) The rôle of opposites polarities in those systems.

133

Polanyi's principal attention has been to how differentiation occurs in the psychic field. Where Gestalt Psychology almost exclusively described the process in terms of Rubin's figure-ground organization, stressing the moment when the *Gestalt* is consciously attained and appreciated, Polanyi speculated about the events leading up to that moment:

> We may say that when we comprehend a particular set of items as parts of a whole, the focus of our attention is shifted from the hitherto uncomprehended particulars to the understanding of their joint meaning. This shift of attention does not make us lose sight of the particulars, since one can see a whole only by seeing its parts, *but it changes altogether the manner in which we are aware of the particulars. We become aware of them not in terms of the whole on which we have fixed our attention.* I shall call this a *subsidiary awareness* of the particulars, by contrast to a *focal awareness* which would fix attention on the particulars themselves, and not as parts of a whole [italics in original].[30]

Normal perception of an object, then, involves being focally aware of that object's total form, and subsidiarily (dimly or semiconsciously) aware of the elements of which it is composed. It is possible to shift one's attention so that the elements of which it is composed occupy the forefront of attention; this detracts from the whole, and in the extreme case eliminates it altogether (as happens when one first sees an unfamiliar object, there is some awareness of the first sees an unfamiliar object, there is some awareness of the disparate details before the overall form is attained. One attends *from* the details to the whole (for example, from the features to the face). Focal awareness reorients itself from the elements to the whole.[31]

This unawareness of the particulars of which our knowledge is composed points to the rôle of intuition and the unconscious in knowing. Polanyi does not make too much of these. Rather, he stresses the dependence of our useful knowledge and skills on

---

[30] Polanyi, Michael. *The Study of Man.* Chicago: The University of Chicago Press, 1959, pp. 29-30.
[31] Polanyi, Michael. *The Tacit Dimension.* London: Routledge & Kegan Paul, 1967, p. 10.

other knowledge that we are not aware of, and cannot express; that is, *tacit* knowledge. Concentrating on the details may disrupt productive thinking about a problem, or performance of a skill. (This is what happened involuntarily to Goldstein's brain-damaged patients.) At the same time, such detailed awareness may prepare the way for improvement of the productive thinking or performance, once attention is again reoriented to the whole.

Polonyi stresses empathy as the content of tacit knowing: projecting one's body into a situation ("indwelling"), or the situation into one's body ("interiorization"). Knowing is inconceivable to him, without something of the knower put into it. When we say that implementable knowledge is based on tacit awareness, and require the knower to conjure up a sort of imaginative fusion of himself and the object of his knowledge, we are at loggerheads with the positivist and the behaviorist, for whom there can be only focal awareness of particulars. Our assertion that science can never be totally objective is reinforced: ". . . suppose that tacit thought forms an indispensable part of all knowledge, then the ideal of eliminating all personal elements of knowledge would, in effect, aim at the destruction of all knowledge." [32]

When the shift is made from the parts to the whole, a shift of levels takes place. The whole may be part of a larger whole that we might come to know by the same means, just as the parts may be composed of sub-parts. That is to say, knowable things are organized into hierarchies, and any given level will manifest qualities that are absent from, and not reducible to the next level down. Every part is interdependent with every other part, and (unlike man-made machines) alteration of one part will affect the entire character of the whole if it affects it at all. This is just as true of living organisms as it is of percepts and concepts. The more complex they are, the more levels they exhibit.

Polanyi explains evolution as partly due to the tendency of entities to arrange themselves in participation in higher forms of organization, which he calls *emergence*. A higher level coalesces out of its own component parts. The parts lose some of their autonomy once the more comprehensive form of organization has

---

[32] *Ibid.*, p. 20.

emerged. The parts do not cause the whole to behave as it does, but the whole exerts a limited control on the parts. Polanyi refers to this subordination by the higher level as the *principle of marginal control.*

A vocabulary for discussing hierarchies, and an interpretation that approximates Jung without too much injection of biased imagination on my part, is provided by Koestler in *The Ghost in the Machine.*[33] An entity that participates in a hierarchy, both a whole and a part depending on what level we attend to, he calls a *holon.* Since a holon is both an individual and a "dividual," and we cannot currently identify the topmost and bottommost layers, hierarchies are said to be open-ended. Physical, biological, and social holons may be part of the same hierarchy. "Whatever the nature of a hierarchic organization, its constituent holons are defined by *fixed rules and flexible strategies* [italics in original]."[34] These fixed rules and flexible strategies are very much like *Gestalt* laws of composition, and "self-actualization." But with the dual, "Janus-faced" nature of the holon comes something new: a conflict of tendencies, an opposites polarity.

> No man is an island—he is a holon. A Janus-faced entity who, looking inward, sees himself as a self-contained unique whole, looking outward as a dependent part. His *self-assertive tendency* is the dynamic manifestation of his unique *wholeness,* his autonomy and independence as a holon. Its equally universal antagonist, the *integrative tendency,* expresses his dependence on the larger whole to which he belongs; his 'part-ness'. The polarity of these two tendencies, or potentials, is one of the *leitmotivs* of the present theory. Empirically, it can be traced in all phenomena of life; theoretically, it is derived from the part-whole dichotomy inherent in the concept of the multi-layered hierarchy . . . *the self-assertive tendency is the dynamic expression of the holon's wholeness, the integrative tendency, the dynamic expression of its partness* [italics in original].[35]

---

[33] New York: Macmillan, 1967.
[34] *Ibid.,* p. 55.
[35] *Ibid.,* p. 56.

At first glance, it would seem that the self-assertive tendency is responsible for man's troublesome aggressiveness.[36] Indeed, spontaneous, transitory outbreaks of aggression are self-assertive. But the great majority of senseless destruction in the world is caused by men in groups, participating in hierarchically organized political and military entities. The *abaissement de niveau mental* of the individual in a collective seems to be merely the principle of marginal control operating at the human level. Of the two tendencies of the human holon, the integrative is the more dangerous.

But if hierarchies come into being so readily and function so smoothly, we might then ask how man comes to be so divided against himself, so fragmented, so dissociated, and so untrue to the topmost layer of his being, his conscious personality? Why do the levels that make him up not reach a working equilibrium, as the other hierarchies in nature do? Koestler (after P. D. MacLean) says this is because man's intelligence burst onto the evolutionary scene so suddenly, and not in response to any particular selective pressure.[37] The lower levels (mammalian and reptilian ones are referred to) are not thoroughly integrated into the hierarchy with man's intelligence at its apex, and retain a dangerous autonomy. Koestler calls this built-in dissociation "schizophysiology."[38] How like Jung's approach it is to view man as torn between opposite tendencies, and in danger of acting out primitive patterns in an antediluvian layer of his psyche, because he cannot integrate them with his conscious attitude!

While there is a good deal more to Koestler's position, I will not attenuate this discussion further. I am not in a position to say to what the parallels between the two men point.[39] He who can, will be the next great luminary in psychology.

---

[36] Most current studies of aggression, be they of the instinctive aggression or frustration-aggression variety, are framed as if that were the case.

[37] See ch. 3.

[38] *Ibid.*, p. 284.

[39] Perhaps we can gain some additional insight by comparing the psychological types of Jung and Koestler. Jung was an introverted, intuitive, thinking type. I judge Koestler to be an extraverted thinking type who is not particularly intuitive. Koestler makes reference to Jung often, but misunderstands him every time a point based on the data of inner experience is in question. Apparently he lacks comparable experiences to draw upon. Koestler comes very close to saying this himself at one point, where he refers to his own "one-sidedness" and "austere Yang" (*Op. cit., The Roots of Coincidence*, p. 141).

# CHAPTER 7

# The Dangers of Analytical Psychology

"I'm glad I'm Jung and not a Jungian." (Personal
communication, Dr. M.-L. von Franz)

If Jung's psychology can be said to have an inferior function, a
troublesome, underdifferentiated, yet vitally important aspect, that
is its practical application. A properly lived human life, in harmony with its own nature, naturally manifests the things we have
covered; but the self-conscious correction of a dissonant life,
even by professional intervention, is a questionable business. However clear our topic's general admonition of openness to that in
oneself which it has become fashionable to ignore or deny may
seem, its specific implementation has a confounding way of going
off the rails. Only up to a point is it possible to alter an individual's
destiny deliberately. The pitfalls along the way to producing de-
sired change in a personality are not obvious.

Jung was well aware of the pitfalls and ambiguities of applied
depth psychology, and therefore avoided the question of an
organized school, with himself and his pupils as proprietors, as
best he could. He said, "I can only hope and wish that no one
becomes 'Jungian.' I stand for no doctrine, but describe facts and
put forth certain views which I hold worthy of discussion."[1] When
he reached his seventies, the only 'Jungian' organizations were
small and collegial.[2] Believing that some solid professional back-

---

[1] Letter to J. H. van der Hoop, January 14, 1946 (Op cit., C. G. Jung:
Letters).

[2] For example, the Psychological Club of Zürich (which occupies the
same building as the present C. G. Jung Institute—Zürich) extended membership by invitation, but was not limited to the holders of any particular
degree or qualification.

ground, preferably medicine, was needed to guarantee the stability and responsibility of a practitioner of psychotherapy, Jung was satisfied to let established channels be the recruiting grounds for psychotherapists. But during that period it became evident that the only alternative to his participation in the establishment of some sort of structure for training psychotherapists, was that one would be established by others, and with worse results than if he were involved.[3] In 1948, the C. G. Jung Institute-Zürich was founded with his approval, and Mrs. Jaffé was its first executive secretary. Other similar institutes have sprung up in London, New York, San Francisco, and Houston. (There is an international organization of graduates of such institutes, the International Association for Analytical Psychology, founded in 1957, with chapters in those and a few other cities.)

The C. G. Jung Institute-Zürich is a modest operation, occupying a few rooms on the upper floors of an old house near the University of Zürich. It confers two levels of credential, the *Propaedeuticum*, a general, non-professional certificate that anyone qualified to attend a university may pursue, and the Diploma in Analytical Psychology, for which an advanced academic degree and 200 hours of approved psychotherapy are prerequisites. The Institute is bifurcated into an English speaking group and one speaking German, and it is possible to complete the entire course using English only. Some excellent courses are given by psychoanalysts and scholars only distantly related to the Institute.

I attended the Institute in the winter of 1970-71. Soon after my arrvial I received the impression that the niveau there must have declined year by year since the death of Jung. Having gone with the intention of staying three years, earning the Diploma, and finding a whole new direction for my career, it was a terrible disappointment to me. I judge the Institute to be worth a summer, or a semester of an undergraduate's junior year abroad. There is nothing about it that would hold the attention of a serious professional, and completion of studies there is no guarantee of competence.[4]

---

[3] Personal communication, Dr. M.-L. von Franz.

[4] I noticed that those with backgrounds in psychiatry and psychology reacted most negatively to the Institute, and I would generally be suspicious

I am really not sure how the discrepancy between the high significance of Jung's psychology and the stagnancy of the world center of its study came about. I can point out some particular areas of difficulty, and describe some revealing critical incidents; I hope by my doing so, that some others who will take up Jung's psychology can be spared reliving the mistakes of the past. Seven categories emerge from my attempt to organize the areas of difficulty, possibly the Seven Deadly Sins of Analytical Psychology.

## 1. The Animus-System

From the standpoint of the philosophy of science, Jung's psychology is a set of heuristic models. The term, "model," is crucial, since it denotes a formulation neither precise enough nor deductively coherent enough to be properly called a theory or a system. The mental pictures called forth by the descriptions of the complex, the archetype, the Ego, etc., are best discarded once an implicit understanding of the inner experiences they pertain to has been achieved; that is, their purpose is largely didactic. The technical formulations exist, like everything in science, to be supplanted by more comprehensive ones that interrelate even more facts.

If mistaken for a bona fide system, Jung's psychology readily becomes a closed system of thought, with a glib answer to every question, a place for everything, and everything in its place. I refer to this closed system as the animus system because it represents a negative manifestation of inferior logos, results from an uncritical, projective fascination, and finds its most intense expression in certain women Jungians for whom Jung as a person gets confused with the animus. One survey of Jung's work, published by one of his close associates with his approval, turned out to be a manifestation of this phenomenon. It made extensive use of pictorial diagrams, accompanied by very confident, positive statements about the "laws" governing the functioning of the

---

of a person in one of those fields who bothered to complete studies there. There are others to whom the Institute represents a way to get into psychology after having had a career in some other field; it is practical for them to complete the course even with misgivings, and they make up the minority of competent people at the Institute.

personality. Since their content is not as systematic as their author made out, the diagrams contradicted one another. For example, in one the unconscious was a small area at the center of a series of concentric circles, in another, the major part of the volume of a cone, and in still another, a sea surrounding islands. Instead of pointing to underlying inner experience, the book provoked the critical reader into picking out the contradictions, and dismissing the whole topic out of hand on their account.

Jung expressed himself on this problem on several occasions. In a letter to Calvin S. Hall,[5] he wrote:

> As I already told you, I object to the term "system." If I had an invented system, I certainly should have constructed better and more philosophical concepts than those I am applying. Take for instance *animus* and *anima*. No philosopher in his senses would invent such irrational and clumsy ideas. When things fit together, it is not always a matter of a philosophical system; sometimes it is the facts that fit together [italics in original].[6]

Much earlier, in 1927, he wrote:

> Analytical psychology is not a *Weltanschauung* but a science, and as such provides the building-material or the implements with which a *Weltanschauung* can be built up or torn down, or else reconstructed. There are many people today who think they can smell a *Weltanschauung* in analytical psychology. I wish I were one of them, for then I should be spared the pains of investigation and doubt, and could tell you clearly and simply the way that leads to Paradise.[7]

## 2. Seeming Broad But Being Narrow

It takes an immensely broad background to be able to put Jung's psychology in context, and avoid the temptation of viewing it as a comprehensive system that accounts for everything.

---

[5] This correspondence pertained to the chapter on Jung in Hall and G. Lindzey's *Theories of Personality* (New York: Wiley, 1954), which is probably the most consulted source on Jung in academic psychology. It is painstakingly accurate, but devoid of the flavor of inner experience Jung's work was about.

[6] November 8, 1954 (*Op. cit., C. G. Jung: Letters*).

[7] C. W., vol. 8, par. 730. "Analytical Psychology and 'Weltanschauung.'"

Since that background includes natural science, psychology, anthropology, and comparative religion to name a few, hardly anybody will have what it takes. Unless one actually exceeds Jung's accomplishment as a generalist, one is limited to a one-sided commentary on him. The present commentary, for example, is strong in General Psychology, but not nearly as strong as I would have liked to be able to make it, in its religious and literary aspects.

The point I am leading up to is not a criticism of dilettantes. There is no harm in being that; indeed, we need more dilettantism to counteract the overspecialization of our times. My point is that many people I saw at the Institute went one step beyond dilettantism. Where the real dilettante pursues things as they appeal to him, the Jungian tries to pursue them as they appealed to Jung, and knows them only from Jung's personal viewpoint. In their hands, Jung's *Collected Works* are mistaken for an encyclopedia of the world's knowledge. I was often reminded of a person who drives through the United States on the Interstate Highways, and then claims he knows all about America.

Since the Institute's specific purpose is training practitioners and researchers, the almost complete ignorance of recent developments in psychology and psychiatry there was shocking. Except for a vague awareness of the earning power of group psychotherapy, the last thirty years of psychopathology and practice was unknown. (One highly respected analyst with whom I took up this point was actually unaware that there was anything beyond the work of Freud and Adler for him to be familiar with!) Psychodiagnostics was limited to a tedious overemphasis on the word association test, and some work with the "tree test," which involves interpreting the way a person depicts the roots, trunk, branches, leaves, etc. of a tree he is asked to draw.[8] Dr. Dora Kalff's work with sand play as a projective technique, going on only a short distance away, was getting to America far more

---

[8] The "tree test" was used in about the same way that American clinicians use the Draw-A-Person test. Because of the obvious possibilities for comparing the same sex and opposite sex figures of the Draw-A-Person test, it would seem to me potentially more useful than the "tree test" in a Jungian context.

quickly than to the Institute. Other projective tests, the Rorschach[9] in particular, that cry out to be radically reinterpreted in the light of Jung's work, received no attention.

To be sure, lip service was paid to furthering knowledge and increasing relevancy of concern, at the Institute. But obvious opportunities to do so went begging.

## 3. The Hero Worship of Jung

An important precondition of narrowness in the Institute people was a preoccupation, or perhaps even fixation, with Jung as a person. This preoccupation had a rather pathetic quality, and was not present in those I met who had been Jung's close associates. There is a yearly ceremony commemorating his death, in which it becomes painfully evident how being a Jungian can become an idolatrous way to express a religious striving.

The worshipful attitude toward Jung is described with stark objectivity by James Hillman:

> The eponym Jungian is more than a common adjective; it evokes the emotional attachment to a man, to a history, to a body of thought and, especially, experience. Some who speak of themselves as 'Jungians' had personal experience with Jung; nearly all have had experience of Jungian analysis. Because 'Jung' continues to play a numinous role in the ideas, dreams and fantasies of Jungians, the term musters psychic energy as an intimate symbol, stirring vital beliefs and feelings of loyalty.[10]

Hillman, who has been associated with the Institute through years when espousing Jung's ideas made one a pariah in any other setting, refrains from making any value judgment about it; he

---

[9] Jung's types formed much of the theoretical basis for the Rorschach ink blot test. The dissociation that exists between Rorschach's method and Jung's concepts apparently stems from the political event of Rorschach's having gone with the Freudians when Jung and Freud parted company in 1913. (See Bash, K. W., "Einstellungstypus and Erlebnistypus: C. G. Jung and Hermann Rorschach," *Journal of Projective Techniques, 19,* 1955, 236-242.) The exciting possibilities of research with the Rorschach taking the archetypal nature of the responses into account, remain virtually untouched. A start has been made by Robert S. McCully (*Rorschach Theory and Symbolism,* Baltimore: Williams & Wilkins, 1971).

[10] "Why Archetypal Psychology?" *Spring,* 1970, pp. 212-217.

describes what he sees. For my own part, the hero worship of Jung goes against the spirit of his work, and nullifies what he intended.

## 4. *Not Knowing What Tolerance Is*

We have already noted the great tolerance and optimism of Jung. While he qualified his optimism later in life, his tolerance was intrinsic to his thought in a rather special way, described by Mrs. Jaffé:

> "Don't interfere!" was one of his guiding axioms, which he observed so long as a waiting-and-watching attitude could be adopted without danger. Situations in which interference was obviously required were decided exceptions. This attitude of Jung's was the very reverse of indolence; it sprang from a curiosity about life and events that is characteristic of the researcher. They happened and he let them happen, not turning his back on them but following their development with keen attention, waiting expectantly to see what would result. *Jung never ruled out the possibility that life knew better than the correcting mind,* and his attention was directed not so much to the things themselves as to that unknowable agent which organizes the event beyond the will and knowledge of man. His aim was to understand the hidden intentions of the organizer, and, to penetrate its secrets, no happening was too trivial and no moment too short-lived. [my italics][11]

This viewpoint, not unrelated to the democratic, pragmatic attitude of William James, has its basis in simple respect for people. It is rather un-European, and that may be why the attempt to carry it on runs into trouble.

At the Institute, Jung's tolerance became translated into a habitual shirking, at every juncture where critical judgment was needed. Whenever I asked a question or wanted to discuss a point with the person who had made it, the other person would discontinue the discussion by saying that maybe another viewpoint was right, and assuring me that mine was respected. It was very puzzling, until someone put me wise to what was behind it. Mutual respect became a reason not to wake the other's mind up,

---

[11] Op. cit., *From the Life and Work of C. G. Jung.*, pp. 102-103.

and the give and take of good discussion was not in fashion at the Institute.

The awareness that thinking is inadequate in many situations, and that literal or logical explanations often turn out to be irrelevant digressions, was also often misapplied in a way that stultified discussion. I recall one lecture where the field theory of Lewin was referred to, and the lecturer, who was in a little too deep, made a terrible mess of it. I asked a few questions, which did not help matters at all, and later made a few suggestions to the lecturer over wine in a café. The lecturer looked at me, uttered the stock phrase, "too rationalistic," and changed the subject. Now it can be very helpful to suggest that a person is being too rationalistic and missing the point when he gets mired in analyzing the explicit meaning of something that has primarily symbolical significance. But that should not be an excuse to avoid taking the trouble to think. Not hindering people can become a bore, if applied so totally that there is no mutual stimulation.

## 5. The What-Imago-Is-It Game

From the flaccid uncriticality of the atmosphere at the Institute, and the tendency there to reject the ambiguity that is necessarily a part of Jung's psychology, one could predict that the interpretation of symbolic material would become a cut and dried affair. This did prove to be the case, and very seldom did discussions about the meanings of dreams, pictures, and so forth go beyond the mechanical application of a few stock devices. All opposite-sex figures were soul representations, and all same-sex ones, the shadow. Every child was a symbol of the Self. Anything appearing on the left side was of the unconscious attitude, and anything on the right side, the persona. Whenever anything appeared three or four fold, it was as if that were the proof positive of everything Jung had ever said. The archetypes of the wise old man, the great mother, the trickster, and the *puer aeternus*[12] provided names and

---

[12] Lit. "eternal child." The characteristics of the *puer aeternus* include a perennial child-like fascination and imaginitivity, avoidance of the commitments of adulthood, and a tendency toward suicide, representing rebirth

stereotypes for a multitude of things. As I heard James Hillman say, the difference between archetype and stereotype is easy to miss.

A particularly humorous example happened in one Institute lecture, where the lecturer, a highly respected senior analyst, commented that it had been his anima that had kept him from preparing lecture notes, so that he would be more spontaneous. (He was one of several who would insist that any unconscious manifestation had to be either shadow or soul as a matter of systematic necessity, and then contradict that proposition any number of times in the same presentation.) I raised my hand, and asked why he thought it was his anima and not his shadow. There was a short gaggle of embarrassed laughter, and a long moment of tense silence. At the next lecture of the series, he mentioned having thought my question over, and was sure it had been his anima. The mere act of giving the phenomenon a name seemed terribly significant to him and, from their generally favorable reaction, most of his audience.

## 6. Isolated Esotericism and Introversion

The Institute attracted quite a few of a certain sort of detached introvert whose only contact with life was as professional therapy patients. They related to their own dreams, fantasies, and transference relationships as detached spectators; their concern with them was esoteric and impersonal. Among them, a conversation might typically start with something like, "oh, I dreamed a wonderful example of a senex (old man) archetype last night." Analysis was a matter of connoisseurship rather than utility with them. Instead of being a means to a more effective life, analysis was life for them. They did not read newspapers, or follow anything that went on in the outside world. They prided themselves on putative superior individuation, and disdained those less withdrawn than themselves as benighted and unconscious. To me, they seemed like refugees from reality, people for whom life's sorrows must have been overwhelming for them to with-

---

rather than death. It is described in detail in M.-L. von Franz's *Puer Aeternus* (New York: Spring Publications, 1970), which does not confuse archetype with stereotype.

draw so completely. I felt like a displaced person among them. It was a bad imitation of Thomas Mann's *The Magic Mountain*, or Solzhenitsyn's *Cancer Ward*.

When analysis degenerates into mere giving names to imagos and phenomena, its essential point is missed. The symbols a person spontaneously produces make a statement about him, his life, and his surroundings, if only we are wise enough to understand it. When an archetype occurs to different people in different places at different times, it does so to express a universal human concern that those disparate people had in common. Even the most obscure symbols in the output of a psychotic person have nothing accidental or random about them. The true purpose of psychoanalysis, more often missed than served at the Institute, is *relation to the individual life of the person* in analysis. Knowing other sources where the particular archetypes have appeared before is useful only because it helps us to understand what the relation is; such knowledge is an adjunct to the essential business of psychotherapy. An esoteric, impersonal attitude toward analysis turns it into something that could not properly be called psychotherapy.

An example from my own analysis while at the Institute illustrates the problem. At the time, I was rigidly resisting the conclusions I was soon to draw from the bad impressions I was receiving. I had a series of dreams, including the following:

> I am back in my childhood home with my mother and father, eating a meal at the kitchen table. My father and I go out to do some errands, and return to find that my mother, who had been complaining of pains, is dead. It is from him that I learn of that. I go by myself to a downtown bank, to collect the contents of her safe deposit box. In it, to my surprise and disappointment, I find a live, unprepossessing, salmon-colored, baby guinea pig in a little cage, together with instructions for his maintenance.

My analyst, who generally showed embarassment at my interest in finding the conditions of my own life and personality in my dreams, pointed out that the pig was an object of worship in some primitive religions (his background was in anthropology). He interpreted the guinea pig as my anima, and said that this

147

showed that the therapy was succeeding, and my individuation was going full speed ahead. He refused to consider that my immediate, spontaneous written description of the dream had made the pig masculine, and then violated one of the few cardinal rules of Jungian analysis by rejecting my own initial reaction to the dream, which was one of apprehension, as having no possible bearing.

During that time, as often happens, the dreams ignored immediate surroundings. By dealing very lengthily with my personal past, particularly my childhood and the home where I grew up, they identified themselves as being about me, but not about any childhood traumas or repressions. The signals were paradoxes, discrepancies between the actual history and the dreams. For instance, at the time of the dream in point, my mother was still alive, and my father had been dead nine years. The behavior of my parents in the dreams was often at variance with the way they had actually behaved. The dreams were actually about my inner development (much of their activity taking place inside the house where I grew up), and my "parents" were representatives of my unconscious, giving sustenance and tutelage, but not without a fearful potential for punishment and destruction. (It would not be wrong to say they were forms taken by the great mother and wise old man archetypes, but no understanding arises from that identification.)

The appearance of the guinea pig after the death of the mother points to a transformation of her into it. The dream pointed to a new direction in my life, tender and rudimentary in form at that point, that was in a way not new at all. It now seems to me that it pointed to my return to the same college teaching job I had come from before my sojourn at the Institute, which would not be the same as it had been. It is not too great an exaggeration to conjecture that the guinea pig is this book, requiring a lot of conscious effort to rear it to maturity.

A few weeks later, at about the time when I first thought of writing this book, I had the last of that series of dreams. I was at my parents' table again, but this time, in my father's place sat Jung (whose speech and mannerisms I knew from filmed interviews), and in my mother's place, Dr. von Franz! That certainly clarified the nature of those enigmatic psychic parents of mine. It also nailed another paradox that had troubled me very much. All along, my dreams had given me evidence that my psyche functioned as Jung described. Yet what my psyche was doing in that manner, was rejecting my experience at the Jung Institute. With lonely irony I adjusted my mind to how limited the circle where these essential ideas are rightly understood, then was.

Looking back, it was probably the connection with the mother, and with nourishment (the recurrent dinner table, as well as the concern of primitive pig worship with nourishment and fertility) that implicitly suggested anima to my analyst. Had he been more sensitive to me as an individual person, he would have seen it long before me. My experience with him, and the few dreams I had about him were all favorable. He was perfectly sincere, but a typical product of very inadequate training. He had had a very competent training analysis, but apparently it never dawned on him that there was a discrepancy between what that analyst did, and what he was taught to do at the Institute.

Even though done in good faith, bad analysis is not harmless. If one fills one's consciousness with spurious interpretations, dissociation increases. The gap between the conscious attitude and developments in the unconscious widens. It is quite conceivable to me that a mildly neurotic person could become very sick, if he were unable to reject the authority of a bad analyst, and kept on trying to force the counterfeit insights of his analysis to fit. When done in a too esoteric and detached way, Jungian analysis produces the same results as any other dogmatic attempt to apply interpretations to people they do not fit.

In my own case, the wish to see my analyst and the Institute in a favorable light kept me on the wrong track for a period of several weeks. The dissociation of my consciousness, busily mulling over false interpretations that could not be integrated, from my unconscious led to a backfire of invasion: I dreamt more and understood my dreams less, until finally, at a particular moment that I still vividly remember, my attitude shifted, I rejected the things with which I had been proccupied en bloc, and all seemed to be put right again. The benefit of my analysis turned out to be a

149

brief first hand experience of what it is like to be acutely neurotic.

Jung was definitely not unaware of the ill effects of spurious analysis, rammed home with the prestige of medical psychology. He surely experienced it first hand during the period when he was trying to wish away his growing doubts about Freud's views. I surmise that Jung's exaggerated optimistic expectation that patients would reject spurious analyses, and his very infrequent mention of the problem, must have covered up immensely strong feelings about it. The one reference to too much reductionism in therapy I recall from his writings concludes: "More than a few suicides in the course of psychotheraputic treatment are to be laid at the door of such mistakes."[13] But his comments in a letter from the "fallow period" after his break with Freud fill the missing pieces in:

> With our patients "analytical" understanding has a wholesomely destructive effect, like a corrosive or thermocautery, but is banefully destructive on sound tissue . . . one can commit no greater mistake than to apply the principles of this technique to an analysed psychology. More than that, all understanding in general, which is a conformity with general points of view, has the diabolical element in it and kills. It is a wrenching of another life out of its own course, forcing it into a strange one in which it cannot live. Therefore, in the later stages of analysis, we must help people towards those hidden and unlockable symbols, where the germ lies hidden like the tender seed in the hard shell. There should truly be no understanding in this regard, even if one were possible. . . . We should bless our blindness for the mysteries of the other; it shields us from devilish deeds of violence. We should be connivers at our own mysteries, but veil our eyes chastely before the mystery of the other, so far as, being unable to understand himself, he does not need the "understanding" of others.[14]

## 7. The Psychotherapist's Shadow

The name of the seventh pitfall is not an invention of mine, but comes from no less a personage than the chairman of the Curatorium (board of directors) of the Institute. In his paper,

---

[13] C. W., vol. 8, par. 678. "Basic Postulates of Analytical Psychology."
[14] To Hans Schmid, November 6, 1915 (*Op. cit., C. G. Jung: Letters*).

"The Psychotherapist's Shadow,"[15] he delivers a prognosis even more somber than mine, on the possibilities of psychoanalysis.

Since the psychotherapist is forced to be an historical successor to the physician,[16] and the religious practitioner, he is prone to manifest their compensatory opposites, the *quack* and the *hypocritical false prophet*. This is to say that the unconscious tendencies to claim as a cure that which is due to fortuitous circumstances he has no control over, and to feign faith in his methods when he himself is cynical and secretly scornful of those who believe, are always latent in him. His efforts are always in danger of being negated by such tendencies.

There was one senior analyst at the Institute who was a living personification of these tendencies. He worked in a small sanatorium run by Jungians, and principally treated acute cases of schizophrenia, claiming to have originated a Jungian method of treating that disorder. From listening to him lecture and reading his book on the subject, I gathered he was simply providing a name for the archetype behind the pathogenic complex, and saying that instantaneous cures came just from that. He made out that the job of the therapist was to instill boundless confidence in the patient by any means that came to hand, so that an essential insight, shot from the hip at some point in the therapy, would "take," with immediate beneficial results.

What he did not point out is that a high proportion of acute schizophrenics get well of themselves, regardless whether they receive treatment.[17] Apparently the illness represents a crisis phase along the way to a new reorganization of the personality in some cases. At no time did he demonstrate a connection between his ministrations and the improvement in those cases that got better, or show that he recognized any need to. The trainees of the Institute, who absolutely lionized and revered him, saw no prob-

---

[15] Guggenbühl-Craig, A. In: Wheelwright, Joseph B. Ed. *The Reality of the Psyche*. New York: G. P. Putnam's Sons, 1968.

[16] Particularly in the prescientific construction of the term implicit in the modern role of the physician, where he is a bringer of transformation, symbolized by the staff and intertwined snakes of the caduceus.

[17] This generalization is based on data so ubiquitously reported in textbooks of Abnormal Psychology that it would be superfluous for me to detail it here.

lem in that. In fact, they merely nodded pleasantly when he would tell them that a psychotherapist was really "the most useless person in the world," or that one had to be either a psychopath or a sufferer from delusions of grandeur, to be a psychotherapist! I later learned, from a staff member of the nearby Burghölzli public hospital, that those who did not get well after a short time at the Jungians' little clinic, were quietly transferred to Burghölzli. This left those who did improve, for whatever reason, to be claimed as cures by that awful doctor.

It was not the man himself, but his colleagues' and students' uncritical endorsement of him, that impressed me. It was part of the same attitude that glorified the worst inequities of patients as desirable manifestations of the Self, or excusable ones of the shadow or the trickster' archetype. So unconcerned was the atmosphere, that it is a wonder that unsavory behavior was as infrequent and transitory in occurrence as it was.

Apparently an idea often illicitly carried over from Freud, that impulse gratification per se is healthy, and obedience to conscience, a bugaboo that therapy is supposed to get one over, had been carried over by the Jungians as an unconscious assumption. Ironically, it was precisely because they tried to ignore those factions in psychology that hold morality to be mostly relative, and presume man to be limitlessly plastic, that the Jungians were susceptible to such un-Jungian unconscious presuppositions. Only in a superficial, intellectualized way was it understood that there is an intrinsic ethical component in man's nature, that he must obey and integrate in order to be healthy.

This contamination of Jung's idealism with naïve moral relativism is shown in the chairman of the Curatorium's analysis, which, as I said, is different from mine, and more pessimistic. He offers, as a sort of corollary law to the compensatory relation of unconscious manifestations to the conscious attitude, the statement that a greater unconsciousness comes with the increased consciousness of being analyzed. In other words, he says that the realization of unconscious potentialities causes further unrealized ones to become active, that otherwise would have remained dormant. This dooms analysts to have more potent shadows than other people, and implies that analysis can never produce a net beneficial result, that it is futile. He finds his own viewpoint captured in the words of a character in Mary McCarthy's *The Group*, a psychiatrist just deciding to change his specialty to brain research: ". . . if you stay, you have your choice of becoming a cynic or a naïve fraud."

The existence of real people who do grow and improve ethically as life unfolds disproves the chairman of the Curatorium's contention. My reading of Jung leaves no doubt that he saw openness to the unconscious as freeing people from the compulsion to live its manifestations out blindly. Every Jungian analyst will tell you that there is an absolute impartiality to the unconscious. Dreams contain a starkly honest commentary on the life of even the most malignantly psychopathic dreamer. The individual personality exists in the context of an inner background that includes and evil as universals.

This means that conscience involves having a standpoint toward the ambivalent, paradoxical condition of good and evil in their unconscious state. Without such a standpoint, their ambiguity might well be mistaken for relativity. But, as the following quote shows, Jung's is a psychology with ethics left in:

> Conscience is a manifestation of *mana*, of the "extraordinarily powerful," a quality which is the especial peculiarity of archetypal ideas. For, in so far as the moral reaction is only apparently identical with the suggestive effect of the moral code, it falls within the sphere of the collective unconscious, exemplifying an archetypal pattern of behavior reaching down into the animal psyche. Experience shows that the archetype, as a natural phenomenon, has a morally ambivalent character, or rather, possesses no moral quality in itself but is amoral, like the Yahwistic God-image, and *acquires moral qualities only through the act of cognition* [second italics mine].[18]

One may ask, after so pessimistic an essay, what now? It appears that educated people in general are becoming more familiar with Jung's work, and that will bring about a welcome reduction in the relative importance of his narrow discipleship. Intercourse with other viewpoints and other fields is unquestionably the solution to

---

[18] C. W., vol. 10, par. 845. "A Psychological View of Conscience."

our seven depressing problems with Analytical Psychology. This means popularization, and while there are drawbacks to that, it is not likely to be worse than the previous period, when Jung's work was frequently maligned but seldom read. At any rate, that you are reading this book shows that interest in its subject is spreading.

In order for my book to expire on an optimistic note, I can point to one favorable development besides the minority of individual analysts who have a genuine vocation for what they do. It concerns Dr. Renée Nell, who guest lectured when I was in my first year of graduate school, and thus was responsible for my first exposure to Jung's work. In those days I experienced nothing in me that corresponded to the shadow, the anima, or the inferior function, and so understood nothing of what she had to say. A few months ago, when I heard she had started a small, controlled milieu sanatorium, applying Jung in a different way, it interersted me very much. Going to Connecticut to visit her represented the completion of a cycle for me.

The members of Dr. Nell's theraputic community are young people who have been unable to adapt outside. Almost all have dropped out of college, and many are accomplished in some kind of artistic work: art, music, or creative writing.[19] In Dr. Nell's words the typical resident "has more insight than he can use. He knows exactly how he should act, but acting is just what he cannot do."

The main emphases of the milieu therapy are psychotherapy that relates symbolic production with the individual situation, and work. The residents themselves see to the basic everyday needs of the household, which represents first steps toward a better relation to their surroundings. These are people with far more vivid inner lives than the rest of us, and for them to make the inner and outer realities complement one another, and not be at cross purposes, is to be cured. The adjustment typical in our society, dissociating inner life to the point that one is not aware that one has such a thing, would be impossible for them. Perhaps to do it that way is where they first went wrong.

---

[19] Nell, Renée. "A New Type of Milieu Therapy." *Journal of Contemporary Psychotherapy*, 1(1), 1968, pp. 37-42.

Theirs is a variation of the central problem of this book, the application of a scientific attitude to the inner reality as well as the outer. For most of us, it is a matter of gaining enough knowledge of the inner to avoid the sad destiny of acting its contents out blindly. That is why false ideologies, putatively based on science, can negate the inner reality and still be believed. Dr. Nell's residents, who are somewhat unusual, would not find that a problem. Mundane reality is the problem for them. We are all affected by the problem of inner and outer in some form; they are another of the sets of tensed opposites that underlie our existence. When one starts to deal with his own unique problem with them, a start toward higher understanding has been made.

# APPENDIX I

Stimulus word list of the 1908 form

Testee . . . . . . . . . . . . .
Tester . . . . . . . . . . . . .
Age . . . . . . . . . . . . . .
Age . . . . . . . . . . . . . .
Sex . . . . . . . . . . . . . .
Sex . . . . . . . . . . . . . .
Date . . . . . . . . . . . . .

| | | |
|---|---|---|
| 1. Head | 29. Bread | 57. Pencil |
| 2. Green | 30. Rich | 58. Sad |
| 3. Water | 31. Tree | 59. Prune |
| 4. Sing | 32. Stick | 60. Marry |
| 5. Death | 33. Sympathy | 61. House |
| 6. Long | 34. Yellow | 62. Dear |
| 7. Ship | 35. Mountain | 63. Glass |
| 8. Count | 36. Die | 64. Dispute |
| 9. Window | 37. Salt | 65. Fur |
| 10. Friendly | 38. New | 66. Big |
| 11. Table | 39. Moral | 67. Turnip |
| 12. Question | 40. Pray | 68. Paint |
| 13. Village | 41. Money | 69. Part |
| 14. Cold | 42. Stupid | 70. Old |
| 15. Stem | 43. Magazine | 71. Flowers |
| 16. Dance | 44. Despise | 72. Hit |
| 17. Sea | 45. Finger | 73. Box |
| 18. Sick | 46. Expensive | 74. Wild |
| 19. Proud | 47. Bird | 75. Family |
| 20. Cook | 48. Fall | 76. Wash |
| 21. Ink | 49. Book | 77. Cow |
| 22. Evil | 50. Unjust | 78. Foreign |
| 23. Needle | 51. Frog | 79. Happiness |
| 24. Swim | 52. Divorce | 80. Lie |
| 25. Trip | 53. Hunger | 81. Decorum |
| 26. Blue | 54. White | 82. Close |
| 27. Lamp | 55. Child | 83. Brother |
| 28. Sin | 56. Attend | 84. To fear |

| 85. Stork | 91. Door | 96. Sleep |
| 86. Wrong | 92. Choose | 97. Month |
| 87. Anxiety | 93. Hay | 98. Pretty |
| 88. Kiss | 94. Satisfied | 99. Woman |
| 89. Fiancé(e) | 95. Scorn | 100. Scold |
| 90. Pure | | |

Translated from *Die Empire des Unbewussten* by C. A. Meier (p. 92)

## APPENDIX II

Translation of letter by Dr. Bally (*Neue Zürcher Zeitung.* Feb. 27, 1934, *Morgenousgabe*, Nr. 343, p. 1.)

Germanic Psychotherapy

Political conditions are forcing the learned bodies of Germany to a reorganization, designated by the term, "alignment" [*Gleichschaltung*]. In substance, this consists of excluding all non-German-national thinking, and all Jewish members.

The General Medical Society for Psychotherapy, too, has been aligned in this way. Its membership has been decimated. Its head, Dr. Kretschmer, found himself obliged to resign. Under the pressure of events, the *Zentralblatt für Psychotherapie*, which for years was published under his proven leadership, had to cease publication from February, 1933. After almost a year it has again been published (December issue, 1933). So long has—so writes the editor, Dr. W. Cimbal—"a continuation of the *Zentralblatt* not been able to occur, because the General Medical Society for Psychotherapy first had to adapt itself to the national revolution and the fundamentally altered form of existence of the German people, before it could again present the work and thought of its researching members in wider circles."

Dr. C. G. Jung (Küsnacht-Zürich) admits to being the publisher of this aligned journal. A Swiss, then, edits the official organ of a society that, according to the declaration of one of its leading members, Dr. M. H. Göring, "assures of all its members active in writing and speaking, that they have read Adolf Hitler's basic book, *Mein Kampf*, with all scholarly seriousness and accepted it as fundamental."

Jung introduces the republished journal with a preface: he asserts that it is the current task of this journal to promote order in the irreconcilable tangle of one-sided psychotheraputic view-

158

points, and "to create a unified view which accounts for the fundamental facts of the human psyche to a greater extent than has been the case heretofore."

No one could refuse to welcome this challenge. Many know that the way to human knowledge leads away from an atomistic-mechanistic conception of the psyche, to a holistic and existential one. Perhaps the journal, under Jung's leadership, will be able, in spite of the current difficulties, to pursue this goal *sine ira et studio* [without anger and without zeal]. Perhaps he would have his influence make of the journal an island of reflection. Possibly he believes he may not wait and must take on the difficult task, mindful that our destiny is bound up with the German spirit. Perhaps he would like to combat the delusion of aryan solipsism, or to preserve the memory, which fundamentally important achievements, for one the psychology encompassing the whole of the psyche and of human existence, Jews and non-Jews, Germans as well as Romans, accomplished through mutual work. In this extraordinary situation, that would have been something for a Swiss to say. But Jung writes: "The really enduring and insightful people long since acknowledged that differences between the Germanic and Jewish psychology should no longer be confused, which can only facilitate science. There is, in psychology more than all the other sciences a personal equation the neglect of which falsifies the results of practice and theory."

What does Jung mean by that? What does he want us to do? Does he want us to ask about a scientific work, is it Germanic or Jewish? How, indeed, does he propose to distinguish Germanic from Jewish psychology? What value would it have for work in the field of human knowledge if we would consider the value of the work of the Jew Husserl "different" from those of Meinong or Dilthey, if we would impose this racial criterion on the works of the Gestalt psychologists of which those of Ehrenfels and Wolfgang Köhler are "German" but those of Koffka and Wertheimer, Jewish? What promise does Jung see in a racial evaluation of the smart concepts of the ethnologist Levy-Brühl, in comparison with the assiduous Frazer? Why does such a distinction seem so important to him that their neglect, as he says, falsifies the results of practice and theory?

Jung reveals to us neither by what means we should accomplish the distinction, nor which specific value we may expect of an attention to the racial in psychology. He promises only: "Thereby, as I wish to state explicitly, no derogatory evaluation of Semitic psychology is meant; just as little is a derogatory evaluation of the Chinese implied when the unique psychology of the far eastern people is discussed."

Why, then, does he not see himself obligated from the outset to say wherein—at last—this so-important value-free distinction between Jews and Germans lies, of which he expects the salvation of future psychotherapy? He owes [us] the answer.

Jung must also withhold the answer. This is self-evident from the situation itself. Whoever imagines himself dealing with the racial question as the editor of an aligned journal must know, that his assertion arises in the context of organized passions, which will lend it the interpretation that is contained implicitly in his words. No, he has already given it. In the same issue, which Jung has signed as the publisher, Cimbal addresses those words; he understood them: "The (next) congress will serve, just as the publisher's preface announces in behalf of the Zentralblatt, for the formulation of a Germanic (deutschstämmig) psychic study and psychic treatment."

What a "value-free" distinction between German and Jewish psychology means for this psychic treatment needs no commentary—Jung calls upon the very destiny that has placed him in this position. This destiny has directed that the National Socialist science policy, thanks to its popularity, can register a success, "although psychotherapy and science have nothing to do with politics."

Dr. med. G. Bally

# Bibliography

Adler, Gerhard and Aniela Jaffé. *C. G. Jung Letters.* Princeton: Princeton University Press, 1973.

Anonymous, "The Therapist as the Self," Unpublished.

Bally, G. *"Deutschstämmige Psychotherapie." Neue Zürcher Zeitung,* Feb. 27, 1934, Morgenausgabe, Nr. 343, p. 1.

Barrett, Lincoln. *The Universe and Dr. Einstein.* New York: Mentor Books, 1957.

Bash, K. W. "Einstellungstypus and Erlebnistypus: C. G. Jung and Hermann Rorschach." *Journal of Projective Techniques,* 19, 1955, 236-242.

Bateson, Gregory, et. al., "Toward a Theory of Schizophrenia," *Behavioral Science,* Vol. 1, 1956, pp. 251-264.

Brome, Vincent. *Freud and His Early Circle.* New York: William Morrow & Co., 1967.

Brown, Roger. *Social Psychology.* New York: Free Press, 1965.

Capek, Milic. *The Philosophical Impact of Contemporary Physics.* Princeton, N. J.: D. Van Nostrand, 1961.

Cassierer, Ernst. *An Essay on Man.* New Haven: Yale U. Press, 1944.

Ellenberger, Henri. *The Discovery of the Unconscious.* New York: Basic Books, 1970.

Festinger, Leon, Henry W. Riecken, and Stanley Schachter. *When Prophecy Fails.* New York: Harper & Row, 1964.

Fromm, Erich. *The Forgotten Language.* New York: Grove Press, 1957.

Goldstein, Kurt. *Human Nature.* New York: Schocken Books, 1963.

Goldstein, Kurt. *The Organism.* New York: American Book Company, 1939.

Green, Hannah. *I Never Promised You a Rose Garden.* New York: Holt, Rinehart and Winston, 1964.

Harms, Ernest. "Carl Gustav Jung—Defender of Freud and the Jews." *Psychiatric Quarterly,* XX(1946) pp. 198-230.

Heidbreder, Edna. *Seven Psychologies.* New York: Appleton-Century-Crofts, 1933.

Hillman, James. "Why Archetypal Psychology?" *Spring,* 1970, pp. 212-217.

Jaffé, Aniela. *Apparitions and Precognitions.* Hyde Park: University Books, 1963.

Jaffé, Aniela. *From the Life and Work of C. G. Jung.* New York: Harper Colophon, 1971.

Jones, Ernest. *The Life and Work of Sigmund Freud,* Vol. 2. New York: Basic Books, 1953.

Jung, C. G., *Analytical Psychology: Its Theory and Practice.* New York: Pantheon, 1968.

Jung, C. G., *Collected Works.* New York: Bollingen Foundation, Inc., 1953 ff. 18 vols.

Jung, C. G. Ed. *Man and His Symbols.* London: Aldus Books, 1964.

Jung, C. G. *Memories, Dreams, Reflections,* Recorded and Edited by Aniela Jaffe. New York, Pantheon, 1963.

161

Jung, C. G., and W. Pauli. *The Interpretation and Nature of the Psyche.* New York: Bollingen Foundation, 1955.
Jung, Emma. *Animus and Anima.* The Analytical Psychology Club of New York, 1957.
Koestler, Arthur. *The Roots of Coincidence.* New York: Random House, 1972.
Köhler, Wolfgang. *The Place of Value in a World of Facts.* New York: Mentor Books, 1966.
Lancaster, Evelyn, and James Poling. *The Final Face of Eve.* New York: Holt, Rinehart, and Winston, 1958.
Leary, Timothy. "The Principles & Practice of Hedonic Psychology." *Psychology Today,* Vol. 6(8), January, 1973, pp. 52-58.
LeBon, Gustave. *The Crowd.* New York: Compass Books, 1960.
Mailer, Norman. "The Prisoner of Sex." *Harper's Magazine,* Vol. 242, (1450), March, 1971, p. 41ff.
Maslow, A. H. *Motivation and Personality.* New York: Harpers, 1954.
Maslow, A. H. *Toward a Psychology of Being.* Princeton: D. Van Nostrand, 1962.
McCully, Robert S. *Rorschach Theory and Symbolism.* Baltimore: Williams & Wilkins, 1971.
Meier, C. A. *Die Empire des Unbewussten.* Zürich: Rascher Verlag, 1968.
Moser, Fanny. *Spuk: Wahrheit oder Irrglaube, Vol. 1.* Baden bei Zürich: Gyr Verlag, 1950.
Nell, Renée. "A New Type of Milieu Therapy." *Journal of Contemporary Psychotherapy.* 1(1), 1968, pp. 37-42.
Polanyi, Michael. *The Study of Man.* Chicago: University of Chicago Press, 1959.
Polanyi, Michael. *The Tacit Dimension.* New York: Doubleday, 1966.
Riesman, David. *The Lonely Crowd.* New Haven: Yale U. Press, 1961.
Royce, Joseph. *The Encapsulated Man.* New York: D. van Nostrand, 1964.
Sartre, Jean Paul. *Anti-Semite and Jew.* New York: Schocken Books, 1948.
Simpson, G. G. and A. Roe, Editors. *Behavior and Evolution.* New Haven: Yale U. Press, 1958.
Thigpen, Corbett H. and Hervey M. Cleckley. *The Three Faces of Eve.* New York: Popular Library, 1957.
Tillich, Paul. *The Dynamics of Faith.* New York: Harper & Row, 1957.
von Franz, Marie-Louise. *C. G. Jung: Sein Mythos in unserer Zeit.* Frauenfeld CH: Huber Verlag, 1972.
von Franz, Marie-Louise. *The Feminine in Fairy Tales.* New York: Spring Publications, 1972.
von Franz, Marie-Louise. *Interpretation of Fairy Tales.* New York: Spring Publications, 1970.
von Franz, Marie-Louise. *Puer Aeternus.* New York: Spring Publications, 1970.
von Franz, Marie-Louise, and James Hillman. *Lectures on Jung's Typology.* New York: Spring Publications, 1971.
von Franz, Marie-Louise. *Zahl und Zeit.* Stuttgart, Klett Verlag, 1970.
Wheelwright, Joseph B., Editor. *The Reality of the Psyche.* New York: Putnam, 1968.
Wilhelm, Richard, Trans. *I Ching or Book of Changes.* Retranslated by Cary F. Baynes. New York: Bollingen Foundation, 1967.
Wilhelm, Richard. *The Secret of the Golden Flower.* New York: Harcourt, Brace, and World, 1962.

# Index

abaissement de niveau mental 24, 93, 137
Abraham, K., 14n
abstract attitude, 127-128
abstraction, 18
active imagination, 39
Adler, A. ix, 13n, 16-17, 29n, 142
Adler, G., 106n, 107
affect, affectivity, 1, 19
Africa, 110-111
aggression, 137
alchemy, 63-65, 79, 81
Allport, G., 122n
ambiguity, 66
Americans, 109-111, 120, 123
amplification, 39
analysis, Jungian, 38-40
"Analytical Psychology," 13n
anima, 43-52, 146, 149, 154
animus, 43-45, 57-58
anti-Semitism, viii, 58, 98-109
anxiety, 127
archetype, 34-36, 43, 65, 67-69, 71, 95, 151; crystalline nature of, 34
Ardrey, R., 35
Aschaffenburg, G.,3
association, free, 39
Astrology, viii, 80, 84
Atlantida, 45
authoritarianism, 15n

Bachofen, J., 112-114
Bally, G., 107, 158-160
Bandra, C., 106
Barnett, L., 77n
Bateson, G., 58n
Baynes, C., 82n
Beatrice, 45
von Beethoven, L., 46-48
behaviorism, 108, 126
belief, 65, 90, 97

Benoit, P., 45
von Bismarck, O., 25
Blacks (Negroes), 31, 109-111
Bleuer, E., 12n
Breuer, J., 3
Brome, V., 13n, 103n
Brown, R., 94n
Burghölzli hospital, 12, 151

Capek, M., 77
Cassierer, E., 15n
Cattell, J., 12
causality, 72, 79, 80
Chakra, 32
charisma, 69
Chestnut Lodge Hospital, 54n
Christ, 30
Christianity, 65, 67, 100
Cimbal, W., 158
Cleckley, H., 54n
Cohen, B., 106
Cold War, 96-99
collective unconscious, 29, 33-34, 70, 99, 100, 102, 109, 119, 120
compensation, 38, 42, 44
completeness, 27, 53n
complex, 1-11, 20, 38, 40, 43, 55, 85, 151
conscious attitude, consciousness, 9, 26, 48, 53, 76, 87, 89, 95, 117
    feminine, 49-50, 119
constellation, 8
contagion, 94, 110
crab, 71
cryptomnesia, 33, 70

Dante, 45
Darwin, C., 37
delirium tremens, 71
delusions, 41, 85; collective, 94
devil, 42

163

dialectical thought, 27n
Dieterich, A., 30n
dilletantes, 142
dissociation, 6, 39n, 55, 69, 117, 128, 149
Dr. Jekkyll and Mr. Hyde, the strange case of, 41
double bind, 58-59
Draw-A-Person test, 142n
dream interpretation, 39, 55-57, 60-61, 71, 125, 132-122, 147-150
drugs, 50, 119-120

Ebbinghaus, H., 3n
ectopsyche, ix
ego, 8n, 26, 49, 93, 96
Ego, 8n, 25-28, 59, 69
Einstein, A., 77
Ellenberger, H., 3n, 103n, 107n, 109n
emergence, 135
empathy, 18, 135
empirical scientific attitude, viii, 65n, 79
encapsulation, 91
endopsyche, ix
Engel, W., 103n
Eros, 16, 45, 48, 50, 111
esotericism, 146-148
ethics, 40, 121, 125, 152-154
"evidence experiment" (Tatbestands experiment), 5-6
evolution, synthetic theory of, 36-38
Existential Psychology, 124
extraversion, 17-18, 92, 137n; forced, 116-119

fairy tales, 117-119
faith, 66
"fallow" period. Jung's, 42
fear, 127
feeling, 19-21, 45, 90-91, 116
feminists, 114-115
feminity, 43, 45, 111-116
Ferenczi, S., 12
Festinger, L. et al., 96-97
Fidelio, 46, 99
field, psychic, 16
figure and ground, 35, 126, 134
focal awareness, 134-136
fourfoldness, 51, 67, 145
Fox, R., 35
von Franz, M.-L., 23, 85-86, 88-89, 120, 138, 148

freedom, 40
Freeman, J., 65
French Connection, the, 41
Freud, S. viii, 3, 8, 12, 13, 15, 16-17, 29n, 33n, 39, 75, 114, 127-129, 142, 150, 152
Fromm, E., 112n, 114, 118, 121, 124-125
Fromm-Reichmann, E., 54n

Galton, F., 3
Garbo, G., 45
Gemeinschaft vs. Gesellschaft, 113n
General Medical Society for Psychotherapy, 102-105
genotype, 37
Germans, 99-109, 158-160
Gestalt, 34, 122, 126-137
Gnosticism, 65
God, 30, 65, 66, 67-68, 96
von Goethe, J., 14n, 17, 45
Goldstein, K., 123-124, 130, 135
good and evil, 40, 47, 66, 67
Gordon, Flash, 96, 98-99
Göring, M., 103, 106, 158
Great Mother archetype, 69, 145, 148
Green, H., 54n
Group, The, 153
Guggenbühl-Craig, A., 151n

Haggard, H. R., 45
Hall, C., 141
Hall, G., 12
hallucinations, 71, 74
Harms, E., 103n
von Hartmann, E., 3n
Hasidism, 106
Hegel, 27n
Heidbreder, E., 126
Helen, 45
hereditary transmission of memory, 31, 34n
hero worship of Jung, 143-144
Hesse, H., 10, 45
Hillman, J., 143, 146
Hitler, A., 101-104, 126
holism, 126, 133-137
holon, 136-137
homologues, 37
Husserl, E., 130
hysteria, 3, 6-7

I Ching viii, 80-83
I Never Promised You a Rose Garden, 54, 58-62
id, 14-15
idolatrous concern, 66, 68
incest, 63-64
India, 120
Indians, 109-111
individuation, 28, 36, 38, 42, 44, 51, 53, 64, 65, 93, 96, 101, 146
industrialization, 113, 117-119
inferior function, 21, 44
inflation, 24, 48
inherited memories, 31, 34
instinct, 36
integrative tendency, 136-137
International Association for Analytical Psychology, 139
introversion, 17-18, 50, 92, 137n, 146-148
intuition, 20-21, 94, 137n
invasion, 24, 69, 117
irrational functions, 20
irrationality, 92, 94
isomorphism, 131
Ixion, 31

Jacobi, J., 107
Jaffé, A., 13n, 85, 86, 107, 144
Jahoda, M., 122n
James, W., 12, 17, 144
Janet, P., 24n
Jews, 99-109, 158-160
Job, 67
Jones, E., 12, 13n, 14n, 106n
Jordan, N., 123n
Judaism, 13-14, 58, 67
Jung, C. G., Institute-Zürich, 138n, 139
Jung, C. G. The Elder, 14n
Jung Codex, 65n
Jung, Emma, 49n
"Jungian", 138, 143

Kalff, D., 142
Kant, I., 3, 34, 78n, 79, 130
Kaufmann, C., 116n
Kerner, J., 33
Koestler, A., 36n, 77n, 133, 136-137
Koffka, K., 34, 122
Köhler, W., 34, 122, 129-133
Krafft-Ebing, 2

Kramer, F., 3
Kretschmer, E., 102, 158

Lancaster, E., 57n
Leary, T., 119n
LeBon, G., 94
Legge, J., 81
Levy-Bruhl, 23
Lewin, K., 130, 145
libido, 8, 18, 41, 62
lie detection, 5-6
Logos, 48, 49, 111, 140
Lorenz, K., 35
love, falling in, 44
LSD, 119-120

MacLean, P., 137
Mailer, N., 114
mana, 153; personality, 69, 101
mandala, 52, 59n, 96
Mann, T., 43, 147
marsupials, 37
masculinity, 43, 45
Maslow, A., 29n, 122-124
mass hysteria, 24, 69, 93-107
mathematics, 87-89
matriarchal principle, 112-118
May, R., 122n
McCarthy, M., 153
McCully, R., 143n
Meier, C. A., 4n, 158
Milt, B., 34n
mind-body conundrum, 71
Mithras, 30
model, theoretical, 140
moods, 48
Morgan's canon, Lloyd, 79
Morris, D., 35
mysticism, viii, 13, 79
myth, 16

national character, 20
native factors, 35-38
natural selection, 37
Naturphilosophie, 36
Nazism, viii, 98-109
Nell, R., 153-154
Neumann, E., 107
Newtonian-Euclidean view, 76-78, 108
Nietzsche, F., 14n, 33n, 42
nirvana, 67n
noise, 116-117

numinosum, 68

objectivity, ix, 19, 129-133, 135
obscurantism, viii, 79
Occam's razor, 79
occult phenomena, viii, 2, 70-91
Oedipus, 57, 106, 112, 114
old age, 53n
opinions, 48
opposites, 17-21, 43, 53, 57, 60, 62, 63, 67, 87, 103, 136-137
paranoia, 41, 69
parliament, 9
patriarchal principle, 112-118
Pauli, W., 78, 87n
Pavlov, I., 35
Perry, R., 130
persona, 24-25, 41, 42, 145
personal unconscious, 33
phenotype, 37
philosopher, Jung as a, viii, 79, 141
physical illness indicated by symbols, 70-71
physics, 69, 76-78, 108, 128-133
Picture of Dorian Gray, the, 41
"pitch-bird," 40n
Plato, 27, 79, 130
pneuma, 44n
Poe, E., 45
Polanyi, M., 16, 133-136
Poling, J., 57n
politics, 92
possession, 43, 102, 116
power, 17
prejudice, 41, 111
projection, 22, 40, 44, 69, 81, 95, 99
psychedelic, viii, 119-120
Psychic elements, 8, 15
Psychic energy, 8-9
Psychic state, 15
psychoanalysis, 13n
psychoid, 78-79
psychokinesis (Pk), 80
Psychological Club of Zürich, 138n
psychosis, 6-7, 52, 61
puer aeternus, 145

racial memories, 34n
racism, viii, 111
rational functions, 19
reflection, 19, 23, 35, 36, 52

religion, 65-70, 79, 91, 112n, 147
repression, 9, 13, 39n
"requiredness," 130
research, quantitative, 80-81, 84-87
resistance, 15n
Rhine, J., 77, 80, 86
Riseman, D., 118
Riklin, F., 4n
risky shift, 94n
Roe, A., 36
Rogers, C., 122n
Rorschach test, 143
Rosenberg, A., 106
Royce, J., 15n, 90-91
Rubin, E., 35, 134

St. Elizabeth's Hospital, 31
Sartre, J., 14n, 108-109
scarab, 76
Schiller, F., 18
schizophrenia, 6-7, 20, 50n, 52, 58
Schlemiel, 40n
Schmid, H., 150
science and humanism, split between, 1, 13-14
scientific attitude, viii, 65n, 66, 69, 79, 155
Self, 8n, 27-28, 59n, 96, 145, 152
"self-actualization," 27, 29n, 122-133
self-assertive tendency, 136-137
senex, 146
sensation, 20-21, 90
Seven Deadly Sins of Analytical Psychology, 140
sexuality, 57, 63, 64
shadow, 40-42, 47, 98, 99, 101, 145, 146, 154; psychotherapists, 150-153
Shakespeare, W., 42
She, 45
sign, 16
Simpson, G., 36n
Skinner, B., 14n
Snakes, serpents, 57, 71, 151n
socialism, 92-93, 107
Solzhenitsyn, A., 147
Sophocles, 112
soul, 10, 42-52, 145, 146
spirit, 36, 43-44, 47, 50, 62, 85-87, 97
squaring the circle, 52
statistics, 84n, 85

166

*Steppenwolf*, 10, 45
Stevenson, R. L., 41
subjectivity, 19
subsidiary awareness, 134-136
suggestion, 33, 39n
suicide, 60n
superego, 8n, 10, 14, 59n
symbolic interactionism, 119
symbolism, 14-16, 27-28, 39, 41, 66;
    contrived use of, 41n
Symonds, J., 119n
synchronicity, 70-91; def., 78, 128

*tabula rasa*, 119, 121
tacit knowledge, 135
Tantaric Kundalini Yoga, 32
Taoism, 80-81
Tavistock Lectures, ixn, 25
teleology, 26-27, 36-38, 126
telepathy, 86n
Thanatos, 17
Thigpen, C., 54n, 57
thinking, 19-21, 90, 137n
Thompson, C., 107
Thorndike, E., 35
*Three Faces of Eve, The*, 54-57
threefoldness, 52, 60, 67, 145
Tiger, L., 35

Tillich, P., 66
tolerance, 144-145
Tönnies, 113n
transcendent function, 27
transference, 40, 57, 62-65
"transphenomenal," 130-133
tree test, 142
trickster archetype, 145, 152
Trinity, 67n
typology, 17-21, 90-91, 137n

UFOs, 96-99
ultimate concern, 66, 68
ultimate reality, 90-91, 92

"value," 130
visions, 72

Welles, O., 96, 97
Wells, H., 97
Wertheimer, M., 34, 122
White, V., 120
Wilde, O., 41
Wilhelm, R., 81
wise old man archetype, 145, 148
word-association test, 3-8, 142
Worringer, W., 18
Wundt, W., 3n, 4

Yin and Yang, 80, 137n